AIR FRYER COOKBOOK FOR BEGINNERS

1200 Days of Simple & Delicious Recipes with Tips and Tricks for Preparing the Best Meals for Every Day

Caitlin Holford

Table of Contents

Introduction

The air fryer is a type of kitchen appliance that allows you to fry food in an oven but with the heat of a microwave. It functions by circulating hot air around the food, and it is typically used for cooking French fries, chicken nuggets, breaded fish, and other similar dishes.

Since their introduction in 2016, air fryers have quickly become the kitchen appliance of choice for many home cooks. Though it is tempting to dismiss air fryers as just another flashy toy, they are actually an excellent tool that can help improve your cooking skills and your quality of life. Food isn't the only thing that can be cooked in an air fryer. You can use them to make fries and even doughnuts.

Air fryers can make a world of difference to those who want to eat healthier. There are so many nutrients that food loses when it undergoes the process of deep-frying, and air frying doesn't suffer from this issue. While there are still a few disadvantages to air fryers, they have still managed to gain a reputation as one of the best cooking appliances you can have in your home.

Air fryers have been featured in popular publications such as NASA's Space Food Lab and a popular cooking show. This is How We Cook. In addition to their widespread use, these contributions show just how much the Air Fryer has been adopted by families across the nation and truly can improve lives all around.

An air fryer essentially does the job of a deep fryer without having to use oil. It circulates cold water around your food and uses an electric fan to make sure the temperature remains comfortable throughout the cooking process. Unlike traditional deep-fries requiring long hours of frying at high temperatures, air fries create crispier food (similar to pan-frying) in only 20 minutes. It also helps to keep your food from getting soggy from being immersed in hot oil. It does not have the same degree of browning as a deep-fryer, but the results are just as good.

Most air fryers have temperature control, which allows the cook to alter the temperature by turning a dial or pushing down a button on its side. Some even have multiple settings that allow you to create different fried foods from one setting, such as chicken nuggets, fish fillets, and other cutlets. To ensure consistent cooking, most models come with an indicator light that shows when the food is ready, even if there is no one in sight, as it quietly circulates food within an enclosed chamber.

In traditional deep fryers, oil circulates very fast, but in an air fryer, the circulation is slower to ensure that the oil does not splash out into the surrounding area. A typical air fryer is about as big as a crockpot and comes in similar designs, such as square and round. The chamber of your air fryer should be able to accommodate most—if not all—of your favorite foods to cook.

Air fries offer a healthier alternative to traditional deep-frying because it limits the amount of oil that you consume at any one time. When you deep-fry, you typically use oil that is 40% or more fat. When you air fry, the oil is only 20% fat. By using the right amount of oil in your air fryer, it will allow you to make healthier dishes with less saturated fat than traditional deep-frying, which uses much more oil.

Chapter 1 What is an air fryer?

An air fryer is a small appliance that allows you to make some foods by frying them in hot air rather than with oil. It's healthier for you because there are no oils or fats needed to cook your food. Plus, all that extra fat creates calories and food that tastes greasy.

Air Fryers are very great for people who are trying to lose weight or eat healthier because it allows you to prepare food that is delicious and healthy.

One great thing about the air fryer is that it's small, so you can take it with you if you want to go camping or away with friends. You can also use it at home because it doesn't take up a lot of room and they're relatively inexpensive.

Another very good thing about the air fryer is that it's easy to use. You just place the food inside of a basket and place it in the air fryer. Then, you set the temperature to what you want and press start or keep it on the heat for 3 minutes. Then, when it's done cooking, you can remove the basket that keeps the food from falling out of the air fryer.

The great thing about using the air fryer is that your food will be crispy on the outside and will still be a bit moist on the inside because of its quick cooking process.

The main downside of using an air fryer is that it limits the foods you can cook. That's because it doesn't have oil or fats in your food, which means you can't use butter or milk to make any pastry, cakes, or bread. If you want to eat dairy, you should use a dairy-free milk substitute instead.

Is it healthy to eat air-fried food?

On the other hand, Air-fried food might be argued to be healthier than deep-fried food because it requires less oil. In comparison to deep-fried French fries, which have a whopping 17 grams of fat per serving, frozen French fries heated in an air fryer have between 4 and 6 grams of fat per serving.

Is it worth investing in an air fryer?

With so many variants on the market, the price of this popular appliance has dropped in recent years—many models are around $200, and others are under $100. Still, buying an air fryer is probably only worthwhile if you frequently prepare fried dishes (frozen or homemade).

What does Air Fryer size one need?

Basket-style air fryers can't hold a lot of food. If you accept this, you and your air fryer will have a lot better relationship.

An air fryer with a capacity of 1.75 to 3 quarts is suitable for cooking meals for one or two people. Also, don't anticipate any leftovers.

Even a big air fryer (four to five quarts) frequently requires batch cooking. You'll probably need to cook a recipe in more than one batch if it serves more than two people.

Consumer Reports discovered that several air fryers' capacity was somewhat less than what manufacturers advertised. This may sound tedious, but keep in mind that air fryers cook food quickly.

Tips to consider while purchasing an air fryer

There are a few things to consider while selecting the ideal air fryer for your kitchen:

Cost

They can cost anything from around $100 to over $500. Pricier models include more functionality, such as pressure cooking or grilling, so you may save money on other kitchen equipment in the long term.

Size

The size of the air fryer you purchase will be determined by the amount of counter space you have available, and you should also assess how many people you'll be cooking for.

Style

Oven-style and basket-style air fryers are the two most common types. Although the oven takes up more counter space, it is more useful and can cook larger amounts of food. Although it normally has fewer functions, the basket drawer type allows you to shake rather than spin the food to scatter it.

Cleaning

Do you despise cleaning the dishes? We recommend choosing a smaller basket because there are fewer parts to wash, and they are easy to clean.

After considering the above, you can select your desired air fryer from a wide range of air fryers that are on the market.

Benefits of an Air Fryer

Air fryers have enjoyed a recent rebound in sales, owing to a greater awareness of nutritional content and a continuing desire for fried foods. Potatoes are consumed more than any other vegetable in the United States, with frozen items such as fries accounting for 40% of total consumption.

When compared to dishes prepared in other ways, deep-fried foods include a lot more fat.

Because air fryers utilize a fraction of the oil that deep fryers use, people can enjoy a healthier supper with the same flavors and textures.

This is perfect because cutting down on one's oil use might be beneficial to one's health. According to studies, dietary fat from vegetable oil has been linked to a range of health risks, including a high risk of heart disease and higher rates of inflammation.

This isn't to say that air-fried chicken is better for you than roasted, slow-cooked, grilled, or pan-seared chicken. A wealth of supplementary equipment is available to produce wholesome and delectable meals. They simply do not have the same fried, crunchy texture as air fryers.

The following are some of the benefits of air frying:

Healthy eating and weight loss

Consumption of fried foods has been related to an increased risk of obesity. This is due to deep-fried foods' high fat and calorie content.

Weight loss can be improved by switching from deep-fried to air-fried foods and avoiding the use of unhealthy oils on a daily basis.

The air fry is fast and convenient

Deep-frying foods make it necessary to use a big container filled with hot oil. This might be dangerous. Although air fryers do get hot, there really is no danger of splashing, spilling, or touching boiling oil by accident. To maintain safety, individuals must use frying equipment carefully and follow the instructions properly.

The air-fried food has the same taste as deep fry food

Air fryers eliminate moisture from foods by heating air containing fine oil droplets, according to studies. As a result, air-fried food has similar properties to fried food but with far lower fat levels.

The Maillard effect is a chemical reaction that occurs when food is air-fried, as it does in many other culinary operations, and it enhances the color and flavor of the dish.

Use less fat and oil

Air fryers use less oil and fat to cook the same food that would require a lot of oil if cooked in the usual manner.

Air fryers pump hot air over a food item to generate the same crispiness as traditional fried foods. Air fryers are able to achieve this by removing high-calorie oil from the food preparation process.

Using only one tablespoon of oil instead of many cups can accomplish the same as a deep fryer but consume a fraction of the fat and calories.

Ease and versatility

Air fryers are easy to use. The manufacturers provide a step-by-step user manual for the individuals to use the air fryer without hassle.

Air fryers are versatile, and it's not restricted to air frying only. One can bake, hydrate, steam, heat, and cook many things using the air fryer.

There are a variety of brands in the market that provide the users with a plethora of additional functions and cooking techniques that an air frying device can carry out.

Reduce the risk of diseases

The development of harmful compounds such as acrylamide can occur when food is fried in oil. This chemical emerges in some meals when high-heat cooking techniques, such as deep-frying, are used.

Endometrial cancer, breast cancer, pancreatic cancer, ovarian cancer, and esophageal cancer have all been related to acrylamide. Additional research has indicated a link between dietary acrylamide and kidney, endometrial, and ovarian cancers, while the evidence is still ambiguous.

By switching to air frying, people can lower their risk of acrylamide contamination in their food.

Cooking with oil and eating fried foods on a regular basis has been related to a number of health issues. To reduce the danger of these outcomes, deep frying can be replaced with alternate cooking methods.

Automatic cooking programs

With air fryers, one doesn't have to learn and follow different methods in order to cook different types of food with varying methods of cooking. Air fryers have various automatic programs that are meant for cooking different types of foods. One doesn't need to be a professional to cook food in an air fryer. It has an automatic system that lets you cook your food by just selecting the function, temperature and time.

Saves the nutritional values of the food

Air frying the food also saves the nutritional value of the food. In an air fryer, less amount of oil and fat is used, and food is prepared by the hot air that is pumped into the device. Although the food prepared is not always of less calorific value, the nutrients of the food are not destroyed in an air fryer. The food cooked is healthy and nutritious. While in the traditional way of cooking, the food that was supposed to be delicious was overcooked on direct heat that is resulting in destroying the nutritional value of the food, whereas in an air fryer, the food is cooked indirectly, just like in case of a convection oven and is not overcooked which in the end preserves the nutritional content of the food.

Chapter 2 User Guide

Before you use any function to prepare your food, note that you shouldn't use kitchen foil to cover any of the air fryer toast oven accessories as it could stop fat dripping to the pullout tray and an accumulation of fat on the kitchen foil could start a fire.

Air Fry Function

Consider crunchier, healthier, and tastier deep fried when you think air fry. The Air Fry feature employs cutting-edge technology that incorporates rapid hot air circulation supported by a high-speed fan and upper heating components, allowing you to enjoy fried food without the guilt of consuming excessive amounts of oil, as is the case with deep frying.

Place the basket in the baking pan and the baking pan on the lower rack position when using the Air Fryer Toast Oven. Select Air Fry and adjust the temperature to your recipe's specifications on the function dial. Set the ON/Oven Timer to the cooking time recommended by your recipe. The power light will turn on, and once the cooking time has passed, the ringer will sound once, and the oven will shut off automatically.

Bake Function

Use the bake option for items that require light baking, such as cakes, muffins, and other pastries. Convection bake, on the other hand, is perfect for bread, scones, pizza, vegetables, and roasts if you want more browning or crunch.

Pizza can be made on a baking sheet, or a pizza stone can be used instead.

Select bake or convection bake and place your rack and baking pan in the appropriate position by your recipe. Set the oven timer to your recipe's time and turn it on. It is advised that you warm your oven for 5 minutes before starting to bake pastries.

The power light will turn on to signal the start of the cooking process. When the cooking time is up, the timer will go off, and the oven will switch off on its own.

Toast Function

Select the toast function and position your food item in the center to ensure consistent cooking.

Place the food items in the middle of the rack and lower them. Pick toast on your function dial and then Toast/Broil to set your temperature. To begin toasting, turn the ON/Toast Timer to the appropriate level of brownness.

The power light will illuminate, and when the cycle is complete, the ringer will sound once before the oven shuts down automatically.

Broil Function

Using the broil feature, broil feature, broiling casseroles, gratins, pies, meats, and vegetables. Convection broiling is ideal for meats and fish because it allows for a deeper browning.

Place the air fryer toast oven basket gently in the baking pan and select Broil or Convection Broil from the menu. Set the temperature to either Broil or Toast. Then, according to your recipe's instructions, turn on the ON/Oven Timer dial and begin broiling. The power switch will be turned on. When the cooking is finished, the timer will sound once, and the oven will turn off automatically.

Note: Do not use glass dishes to broil.

Warm Function

Set your temperature to warm, and choose warm on your function dial while placing the baking pan or oven rack on the bottom rack position. After that, set your ON/Oven Timer to the desired duration. When the timer you set expires, the power light will turn on, and the ringer will turn off. The oven will shut down on its own.

Cleaning and Maintenance of Air Fryer

Pull out the pan and the basket from the unit

Immediately the appliance is cooled off, remove the pan and cooking basket. This is very important, and you have to place the basket on a few pieces of paper towel to catch any grease coming out from the component.

Get rid of the grease coming out from the bottom of the pan

When there is grease deposited in the bottom of the pan, remove them before you begin washing the appliance. You may also place the component in a container such as a plastic tub or glass jar and then remove the grease into the jar. Discard and seal up the container immediately you get rid of the grease.

Soak the pan and basket in hot and soapy water

This is to help remove any sticky residue from the basket. Fill up the pan with hot water and dish soap. Nest the cooking basket inside the pan, allow them to soak in the water for at least 10 minutes.

Rub down the outside with a wet cloth

While you are cooking, there could be some stains on the body of the Air Fryer from your fingers. Use a light wet cloth to wipe the outside body of the unit. Clean the buttons and handle. It is also good to apply a little amount of grease-remover solution onto your fabric and use it to scrub away any stubborn spots.

Clean out the inner chamber along with the heating element. Do not use a hard sponge. Use a damp sponge in hot soapy water. To clean the heating element, turn the unit upside down to enable you to see it clearly. Scrub the surface of the coil to release the greasy residue.

Disconnect Your Air Fryer from Its Power Source

This is the first safety measure you do before you start cleaning the unit. Make sure to unplug the appliance from electricity after every use and then wait for at least 30 minutes to let it cool off. When it is completely cool off, you can start washing the unit. From time to time, you may not have sufficient time to wait for the unit to cool off; it's advisable to wear a heat-resistance hand cloves beef handling the hot unit.

Dry up the pan and basket before reinserting into the Air Fryer

Once you are through with the cleaning process, set them out to air-dry for about 30 to 60 minutes using a paper towel to get rid of any excess water. When they are completely dry, fix the basket into the pan and then set the pan into the body of the Air Fryer.

Tips & tricks

Air fryers are designed to be super easy to use. Here's a little guide to get you started.

Choose a recipe

Choose a recipe that you can cook in your air fryer. Remember that most foods that you cook in your microwave or oven or on the stovetop can be prepared in the air fryer—except for those recipes that have a lot of fat or liquids. You can use my air fryer cookbook to help you find suitable recipes.

Prepare the air fryer

Read through the recipe to the end so you know what accessories you need for cooking. Some recipes call for using the basket, rack, or rotisserie that comes with the air fryer. Other recipes use cake or muffin pans that you can insert into the air fryer. Just be sure these pans fit into the fryer and are safe to use.

Prepare the ingredients

Gather the ingredients for the recipe and prep them according to the instructions. When prepped, put the ingredients into the air fryer or in the basket, rack, or pans within the air fryer. Use parchment baking paper or a light mist of oil spray to prevent food from sticking.

Never crowd food in the air fryer or over-fill. Food that is loaded in the air fryer won't cook evenly and can be raw and undercooked. You may have to cook more than one batch if you're preparing for a crowd.

Setting the temperature and time

Check the recipe for the correct temperature and time setting. You can set it manually or use the digital setting for the temperature and time needed for the recipe. Most air fryers also have preset functions that make them easy to set according to each recipe.

Check food during cooking

Many air fryer recipes require you to check the food while it's cooking to cook evenly and not over-cook. All you have to do is shake, flip, or toss the food to distribute it. Or, for some recipes, you'll need to turn the food about halfway through when cooking so that it cooks and crisps all the way thoroughly around.

Cleaning the air fryer

Once the food is cooked, remove and unplug the air fryer. Let it cool completely before cleaning. Stick to the directions that go with the fryer for proper cleaning. Never scrub or use abrasive cleaners when cleaning the fryer or the fryer accessories. What air fryer should you use?

The recipes in this book can be used with any model of an air fryer. This includes oven-style fryers with horizontal racks or fryers with a basket and handle.

Using the basket or rack

Some models of air fryers use a round basket where foods are cooked, while other models will have layered racks that fit into a square cooking space, much like a small oven. My recipes can be used for both baskets and racks.

Keep an eye on timing

You'll find that air fryers cook at different temperatures depending on what model you have. This is why it's essential to check on foods during the cooking process, so you don't over or undercook them. If you've cut back on quantities in some of my recipes, be sure to cut the cooking time down accordingly. Remember, my hints are just recommendations to guide you as you use your air fryer.

Using oil sprays

Several recipes from this book use a lot of oil spray—I use PAM. But you can use any brand you want. Or make your own by merely putting olive oil into a small spray bottle. Use a small amount of oil and spray over the basket and trays to prevent food from sticking. Some of my recipes require you to spray the food with oil directly.

Additional Tips

Warm-up your Air Fryer

It is standard to always preheat your cooking item and make it a regular habit. Oftentimes, people do it, sometimes they don't do it, and my meal is still good. For instance, if your air fryer does not have any preheat feature, simply turn it to the preferred temperature and allow it to run for about 3 minutes before bringing adding the food.

Use Oil to Cook Foods in the Air Fryer

All of us prefer using oils for certain foods to make them crunchier, but other foods don't always need it.

Don't Put Too Much in the Basket

If you would like your fried food to turn out to be delicious and fresh, you'll need to ensure you don't block the appliance. Putting too much food in the bowl will keep the food from browning and stretching. Cook your food in Tupperware or invest in a larger air fryer to make sure this doesn't happen.

Shake it During Frying and Other Cooking

Upon frying small items like French fries and chicken wings, shake the basket every few minutes to guarantee uniform cooking; sometimes, instead of tossing, use a couple of silicone kitchen pins to turn over more essential items.

Chapter 3. Breakfast

1. Banana Bread Pudding

Intermediate Recipe

Preparation Time: 10 minutes

Cooking Time: 20 minutes

Serving: 4

Ingredients:

- Olive oil
- 2 medium ripe bananas, mashed
- ½ cup low-fat milk
- 2 tablespoons peanut butter
- 2 tablespoons maple syrup
- 1 teaspoon ground cinnamon
- 1 teaspoon vanilla extract
- 2 slices whole-grain bread, torn into bite-sized pieces
- ¼ cup quick oats

Directions:

1. Lightly spray four individual ramekins or one air fryer-safe baking dish with olive oil.
2. In a large mixing bowl, combine the bananas, milk, peanut butter, maple syrup, cinnamon, and vanilla. Using an electric mixer or whisk, mix until fully combined.
3. Add the bread pieces and stir to coat in the liquid mixture.
4. Add the oats and stir until everything is combined.
5. Transfer the mixture to the baking dish or divide between the ramekins. Cover with aluminum foil.
6. Place 2 ramekins in the fryer basket and air fry until heated through, 10 to 12 minutes.
7. Remove the foil and cook for 6 to 8 more minutes.
8. Repeat with the remaining 2 ramekins. Make It Even Lower Calorie: Reduce the calories by using sugar-free maple syrup or by replacing the peanut butter with PB2 (powdered peanut butter). Combine 4 tablespoons of powdered peanut butter with 2 tablespoons of water to equal 2 tablespoons of peanut butter.

Nutrition:

- Calories: 212 kcal
- Fat: 6 g
- Saturated Fat: 2 g
- Carbs: 38 g
- Protein: 6 g
- Sodium: 112 mg

2. Air fried German Pancakes

Basic Recipe

Preparation Time: 5 minutes

Cooking Time: 8 Minutes

Serving: 5

Ingredients:

- erving size: 1/2 cup batter
- 3 Full eggs
- Whole wheat flour: 1 cup
- Almond milk: 1 cup
- A salt pinch
- Apple sauce: 2 heaping tablespoons (optional but recommended to replace the need for added oil or butter)

For Garnishing:

- Berries
- Greek yogurt
- Confectioner sugar
- Maple syrup (optional)

Directions:

1. Set the air fryer temperature to 390°F/199°C. Inside the air fryer, set the cast iron tray or ramekin as it heats. Take the blender and add all the batter ingredients to it, and combine until smooth. If the batter is too thick, simply add milk or applesauce tablespoons to smooth out. Use the nonstick baking spray and spray the cast iron tray or ramekin, and then dump in a batter serving.
2. Air fry the batter for 6-8 minutes
3. Do not worry if the top gets hard to touch. This is the advantage of using the air fryer—it provides the pancake with a good firm outer coating/edges that softens as it cools. Place the remaining batter in the refrigerator in an airtight container to freshen it up every morning.
4. Garnish, and serve.

Nutrition:

- Calories: 139 kcal
- Protein: 8 g
- Fat: 4 g
- Carbs: 18 g
- Fiber: 3 g
- Sugar: 1 g

3. Air-Fried Flax Seed French toast Sticks with Berries

Intermediate Recipe
Preparation Time: 25 minutes
Cooking Time: 35 minutes
Serving: 4

Ingredients:

- Whole-grain bread: 4 slices (1 1/2-oz)
- 2 Big Eggs
- 1/4 cup 2% reduced-fat milk
- Vanilla extract: 1 teaspoon
- Ground cinnamon: ½ teaspoon
- 1/4 cup of light brown sugar, split,
- 2/3 cup flax seed cooking spray
- 2 Cups of fresh-cut strawberries
- Maple syrup: 8 teaspoons
- Powdered sugar: 1 teaspoon

Directions:

1. Cut each of the bread slices into four long sticks. In a shallow dish, whisk together eggs, milk, cinnamon, vanilla extract, and 1 tablespoon brown sugar. In a second, shallow dish, combine the flaxseed meal and the remaining 3 tablespoons of brown sugar.
2. Dip the pieces of bread in a mixture of eggs, soak them slightly, and allow any excess to drip away. Dredge each piece in a mixture of flax seeds and coat on all sides. Cover the bits of bread with cooking oil.
3. Place pieces of bread in a single layer in the air fryer basket, leave room between each piece and cook at 375°F in batches until golden brown and crunchy, 10 minutes, turn slices over halfway through cooking. Place 4 sticks of French toast on each plate to serve. Finish with 1/2 cup of strawberries, 2 teaspoons of maple syrup, and a powdered sugar layer. Serve right now.

Nutrition:

- Calories: 361 kcal
- Fat: 10 g
- Saturated Fat: 1 g
- Unsaturated Fat: 7 g
- Protein: 14 g
- Carbs: 56 g
- Fiber: 10 g
- Sugars: 30 g
- Sodium: 218 mg

4. Breakfast Frittatas

Basic Recipe

Preparation Time: 15 minutes

Cooking Time: 20 minutes

Serving: 2

Ingredients:

- Breakfast sausage: ¼ pound, completely cooked and crumbled
- Eggs: 4, lightly beaten
- Shredded cheddar cheese: ½ cup
- Red pepper: 2 tablespoons, chopped
- G
reen onion: 1 chopped
- Cayenne pepper: 1 pinch
- Cooking spray

Directions:

1. Combine the sausage, eggs, cheddar cheese, onion, bell pepper, and cayenne in a bowl and blend. Set the temperature of the air-fryer to 360°F (180°C). Sprinkle a 6x2-inch non-stick cake pan with a cooking spray.
2. Put the mixture of the eggs in the prepared cake pan. Cook in the air fryer for 18 to 20 minutes until the frittata is set.

Nutrition:

- Calories: 379.8 kcal
- Protein: 31.2 g
- Carbs: 2.9 g
- Cholesterol: 443 mg
- Sodium: 693.5 mg

5. Air-Fried Breakfast Bombs

Basic Recipe

Preparation Time: 20 minutes

Cooking Time: 5 minutes

Serving: 2

Ingredients:

- Bacon: 3 slices, center-cut
- 3 Big, lightly beaten eggs
- 1 1/3-ounce fat cream cheese, softened
- Fresh chives: 1 tablespoon, chopped
- 4 Ounces new whole wheat flour pizza dough
- Cooking spray

Directions:

1. Cook the bacon over medium to very crisp in a medium skillet, around 10 minutes. Take bacon off the pan. In a pan, add eggs to the bacon drippings; cook for about 1 minute, frequently stirring, until almost set but still loose. Transfer eggs to a bowl; add cream cheese, chives, and crumbled bacon to taste.
2. Divide the dough into four pieces equal to each. Roll each piece into a 5-inch circle onto a lightly floured surface—place one-fourth of each dough circle in the middle of the egg mixture. Brush the outside edge of the dough with water; wrap the dough around the mixture of the eggs to form a bag, pinch the dough at the seams together.
3. In the air fryer tray, put dough bags in a single layer; coat thoroughly with cooking spray. Cook for 5 to 6 minutes at 350°F until golden brown, then test for 4 minutes

Nutrition:

- Calories: 305 kcal
- Fat: 15 g
- Saturated Fat: 5 g
- Unsaturated Fat: 8 g
- Protein: 19 g
- Sodium: 548 mg
- Calcium: 5 %
- DV Potassium: 2% DV
- Carbs: 26 g
- Fiber: 2 g
- Sugars: 1 g
- Added sugars: 0 g

6. Banana Bread

Basic Recipe

Preparation Time: 5 minutes

Cooking Time: 30 minutes

Serving: 4

Ingredients:

- Banana: 1, ripe and mashed
- 1 egg
- Brown sugar: 2-3 tablespoons
- Canola oil: 2 tablespoons
- Milk: 1/4 cup
- Plain flour: ¾ cup mixed with 1/2 tablespoon baking soda

Directions:

1. Whisk the egg into the mashed banana in a small bowl. Add the sugar, butter, and milk and whisk again.
2. Add the flour and baking soda to the mixture and blend until mixed.
3. If using an air fryer, preheat for 3 minutes to 320°F/160°C.
4. Pour the batter into the dish of the air fryer (apply a little butter on the basket) and cook for 32 to 35 minutes, or until a toothpick inserted into the cake's bottom comes out clean. A touch of stickiness is all right.
5. Let the tin/dish cool for 10 minutes, then transfer to a wire rack to cool down.

Nutrition:

- Calories: 233 kcal
- Sodium: 25 mg
- Protein: 5 g
- Fat: 9 g
- Carbs: 34 g
- Sugar: 13 g
- Saturated Fat: 1 g
- Potassium: 178 mg
- Fiber: 1 g
- Vitamin A: 105 IU
- Cholesterol: 42 mg
- Vitamin C: 2.6 mg
- Calcium: 34 mg
- Iron: 1.4 m

7. Sausage Breakfast Casserole

Intermediate Recipe

Preparation Time: 10 minutes

Cooking Time: 20 minutes

Serving: 6

Ingredients:

- Hash browns: 1 Lb.
- Breakfast Sausage: 1 lb.
- Eggs: 4
- Green Bell Pepper: 1, diced
- Red Bell Pepper: 1, diced
- Yellow Bell Pepper: 1, diced
- Sweet onion: ¼ cup, diced

Directions:

1. Cover the air fryer basket lined with foil. Put the hash browns on the bottom basket of the air fryer.
2. Place the uncooked sausage over it.

3. Place the peppers and the onions evenly on top.
4. Cook it for 10 minutes at 355°F.
5. When needed, open the air fryer and mix the casserole up a bit.
6. Whisk each egg in a bowl, and then pour right over the saucepan.
7. Cook another 10 minutes on 355°F.
8. Serve with a sprinkle of salt and pepper.

Nutrition:

- Calories: 517 kcal
- Fat: 37 g
- Saturated Fat: 10 g
- Trans Fat: 0 g
- Unsaturated Fat: 25 g
- Cholesterol: 189 mg
- Sodium: 1092 mg
- Carbs: 27 g
- Fiber: 3 g
- Sugar: 4 g
- Protein: 21 g

8. Breakfast Burritos

Basic Recipe

Preparation Time: 20 minutes

Cooking Time: 3 minutes

Serving: 8

Ingredients:

- Breakfast sausage: 1 pound
- 1 Chopped bell pepper
- Eggs: 12, lightly beaten
- Black pepper: ½ teaspoon
- Sea salt: 1 teaspoon
- Flour tortillas: 8 (burrito style)
- Shredded cheddar cheese: 2 cups

Directions:

1. Crumble and cook the sausage until brown in a large skillet. Add chopped peppers. Dry out grease, put the sausage on a towel-lined sheet of paper, cover it, and set it aside.
2. Melt 1 spoonful of butter in a large saucepan, add eggs, salt, and pepper and cook over medium heat, stirring continuously until almost set and no longer runny.
3. Remove from heat and whisk in cooked sausage.
4. In the center of a tortilla, add some of the egg and sausage mixtures, top with some of the bacon, fold sides, and roll up. Preheat the fryer until 390°F.
5. Spray burritos gently with a drop of olive oil. Place as many burritos as fit into the air fryer and cook for 3 minutes at 390°F, rotating trays halfway through. Cook extra for 3 minutes for crispier burritos. Immediately remove and serve, or allow cooling slightly, then wrapping well and freezing for meal preparation.

Nutrition:

- Calories: 283 kcal
- Carbs: 16 g
- Fat: 17 g
- Protein: 16 g

9. Breakfast Burritos

Intermediate Recipe

Preparation Time: 10 minutes

Cooking Time: 12 Minutes

Serving: 2

Ingredients:

- 2 eggs
- 1 tablespoon chives, fresh, chopped
- ½ teaspoon paprika
- ½ teaspoon cayenne pepper
- 3-ounces cheddar cheese, shredded
- ½ teaspoon butter
- ¼ teaspoon salt
- 4-ounces bacon, cut into tiny pieces

Directions:

1. Slice bacon into tiny pieces and sprinkle it with cayenne pepper, salt, and paprika. Mix the chopped bacon.
2. Spread butter in the bottom of ramekin dishes and beat the eggs there. Add the chives and shredded cheese.
3. Add the chopped bacon over the egg mixture in ramekin dishes. Place the ramekins in your air fryer basket.
4. Preheat your air fryer to 360°F. Place the air fryer basket in your air fryer and cook for 12-minutes. When the cooking time is completed, remove the ramekins from the air fryer and serve warm.

Nutrition:

- Calories: 553 kcal
- Fat: 43.3 g
- Carbs: 2.3 g
- Protein: 37.3 g

10 Breakfast Chicken Strips

Intermediate Recipe

Preparation Time: 10 minutes

Cooking Time: 12 minutes

Serving: 4

Ingredients:

- 1 teaspoon paprika
- 1 tablespoon cream
- 1 lb. chicken fillet
- ½ teaspoon salt
- ½ teaspoon black pepper

Directions:

1. Cut the chicken fillet into strips. Sprinkle the chicken fillets with salt and pepper.
2. Preheat the air fryer to 365°F.
3. Place the butter in the air basket tray and add the chicken strips. Cook the chicken strips for 6-minutes
4. Turn the chicken strips to the other side and cook them for an additional 5-minute after strips are cooked. Sprinkle them with cream and paprika, then transfer them to serving plates.
5. Serve warm.

Nutrition:

- Calories: 245 kcal
- Fat: 11.5 g
- Carbs: 0.6 g
- Protein: 33 g

11. No-Bun Breakfast Bacon Burger

Intermediate Recipe

Preparation Time: 10 minutes

Cooking Time: 8 minutes

Serving: 2

Ingredients:

- 8-ounces ground beef
- 2-ounces lettuce leaves
- ½ teaspoon minced garlic
- 1 teaspoon olive oil
- ½ teaspoon sea salt
- 1 teaspoon ground black pepper
- 1 teaspoon butter
- 4-ounces bacon, cooked
- 1 egg
- ½ yellow onion, diced
- ½ cucumber, slice finely
- ½ tomato, slice finely

Directions:

1. Begin by whisking the egg in a bowl, then add the ground beef and combine well.
2. Add cooked, chopped bacon to the ground beef mixture.
3. Add butter, ground black pepper, minced garlic, and salt.
4. Mix and make burgers.
5. Preheat your air fryer to 370°F.
6. Spray the air fryer basket with olive oil and place the burgers inside of it.
7. Cook the burgers for 8-minutes on each side. Meanwhile, slice the cucumber, onion, and tomato finely.

8. Place the tomato, onion, and cucumber onto the lettuce leaves.
9. When the burgers are cooked, allow them to chill at room temperature, and place them over the vegetables and serve.

Nutrition:

- Calories: 618 kcal
- Fat: 37.8 g
- Carbs: 8.6 g
- Protein: 59.4 g

12. Breakfast Coconut Porridge

Intermediate Recipe

Preparation Time: 5 minutes

Cooking Time: 7 minutes

Serving: 4

Ingredients:

- 1 cup coconut milk
- 3 tablespoons blackberries
- 2 tablespoons walnuts
- 1 teaspoon butter
- 1 teaspoon ground cinnamon
- 5 tablespoons chia seeds
- 3 tablespoons coconut flakes
- ¼ teaspoon salt

Directions:

1. Pour the coconut milk into the air fryer basket tray. Add the coconut, salt, chia seeds, ground cinnamon, and butter.
2. Ground up the walnuts and add them to the air fryer basket tray. Sprinkle the mixture with salt.
3. Mash the blackberries with a fork and add them also to the air fryer basket tray.
4. Cook the porridge at 375°F for 7-minutes when the cooking time is over, remove the air fryer basket from the air fryer and allow sitting and resting for 5-minutes Stir porridge with a wooden spoon and serve warm.

Nutrition:

- Calories: 169 kcal
- Fat: 18.2 g
- Carbs: 9.3 g
- Protein: 4.2 g

Chapter 4 Meat

13. Juicy Pork Chops

Basic Recipe

Preparation Time: 10 minutes

Cooking Time: 16 minutes

Servings: 4

Ingredients:

- 4 pork chops, boneless
- 2 teaspoon olive oil
- ½ teaspoon celery seed
- ½ teaspoon parsley
- ½ teaspoon granulated onion
- ½ teaspoon granulated garlic
- ¼ teaspoon sugar
- ½ teaspoon salt

Directions:

1. In a small bowl, mix together oil, celery seed, parsley, granulated onion, granulated garlic, sugar, and salt.
2. Rub seasoning mixture all over the pork chops.
3. Place pork chops on the air fryer oven pan and cook at 350°F for 8 minutes
4. Turn pork chops to the other side and cook for 8 minutes more.
5. Serve and enjoy.

Nutrition:

- Calories: 279 kcal
- Fat: 22.3 g
- Carbs: 0.6 g
- Protein: 18.1 g

14. Crispy Meatballs

Basic Recipe

Preparation Time: 10 minutes

Cooking Time: 12 minutes

Servings: 8

Ingredients:

- 1 lb. ground pork
- 1 lb. ground beef
- 1 tablespoon Worcestershire sauce
- ½ cup feta cheese, crumbled
- ½ cup breadcrumbs
- 2 eggs, lightly beaten
- ¼ cup fresh parsley, chopped
- 1 tablespoon garlic, minced
- 1 onion, chopped
- ¼ teaspoon pepper
- 1 teaspoon salt

Directions:

1. Add all the ingredients into the mixing bowl and mix until well combined.
2. Spray air fryer oven tray pan with cooking spray.
3. Make small balls from meat mixture and arrange on a pan and air fry t 400°F for 10-12 minutes
4. Serve and enjoy.

Nutrition:

- Calories: 263 kcal
- Fat: 9 g
- Carbs: 7.5 g
- Protein: 35.9 g

15. Flavorful Steak

Basic Recipe

Preparation Time: 10 minutes

Cooking Time: 18 minutes

Servings: 2

Ingredients:

- 2 steaks, rinsed and pat dry
- ½ teaspoon garlic powder
- 1 teaspoon olive oil
- Pepper
- Salt

Directions:

1. Rub steaks with olive oil and season with garlic powder, pepper, and salt.
2. Preheat the instant vortex air fryer oven to 400°F.
3. Place steaks on air fryer oven pan and air fry for 10-18 minutes, turning halfway through.
4. Serve and enjoy.

Nutrition:

- Calories: 361 kcal
- Fat: 10.9 g

- Carbs: 0.5 g
- Protein: 61.6 g

16. Easy Rosemary Lamb Chops

Basic Recipe

Preparation Time: 10 minutes

Cooking Time: 6 minutes

Servings: 4

Ingredients:

- 4 lamb chops
- 2 tablespoon dried rosemary
- ¼ cup fresh lemon juice
- Pepper
- Salt

Directions:

1. In a small bowl, mix together lemon juice, rosemary, pepper, and salt. Brush lemon juice rosemary mixture over lamb chops.
2. Place lamb chops on air fryer oven tray and air fry at 400°F for 3 minutes. Turn lamb chops to the other side and cook for 3 minutes more. Serve and enjoy.

Nutrition:

- Calories: 257 kcal
- Fat: 22.7 g
- Carbs: 1.4 g
- Protein: 16.9 g

17. BBQ Pork Ribs

Basic Recipe

Preparation Time: 10 minutes

Cooking Time: 12 minutes

Servings: 6

Ingredients:

- 1 slab baby back pork ribs, cut into pieces
- ½ cup BBQ sauce
- ½ teaspoon paprika

- Salt

Directions:

1. Add pork ribs to a mixing bowl. Add BBQ sauce, paprika, and salt over pork ribs and coat well, and set aside for 30 minutes
2. Preheat the instant vortex air fryer oven to 350°F. Arrange marinated pork ribs on an instant vortex air fryer oven pan and cook for 10-12 minutes. Turn halfway through.
3. Serve and enjoy.

18. Herb Butter Rib-eye Steak

Basic Recipe

Preparation Time: 10 minutes

Cooking Time: 14 minutes

Servings: 4

Ingredients:

- 2 lb rib eye steak, bone-in
- 1 teaspoon fresh rosemary, chopped
- 1 teaspoon fresh thyme, chopped
- 1 teaspoon fresh chives, chopped
- 2 teaspoons fresh parsley, chopped
- 1 teaspoon garlic, minced
- ¼ cup butter softened
- Pepper
- Salt

Directions:

1. In a small bowl, combine together butter and herbs.
2. Rub herb butter on rib-eye steak and place it in the refrigerator for 30 minutes.
3. Place marinated steak on instant vortex air fryer oven pan and cook at 400°F for 12-14 minutes.
4. Serve and enjoy.

Nutrition:

- Calories: 416 kcal
- Fat: 36.7 g
- Carbs: 0.7 g
- Protein: 20.3 g

19. Classic Beef Jerky

Basic Recipe

Preparation Time: 10 minutes

Cooking Time: 4 hours

Servings: 4

Ingredients:

- 2 lb London broil, sliced thinly
- 1 teaspoon onion powder
- 3 tablespoon brown sugar
- 3 tablespoon soy sauce
- 1 teaspoon olive oil
- 3/4 teaspoon garlic powder

Directions:

1. Add all the ingredients except meat in the large zip-lock bag.
2. Mix until well combined. Add the meat to the bag.
3. Seal bag and massage gently to cover the meat with marinade.
4. Let marinate the meat for 1 hour.
5. Arrange marinated meat slices on an instant vortex air fryer tray and dehydrate at 160°F for 4 hours.

Nutrition:

- Calories: 133 kcal
- Fat: 4.7 g
- Carbs: 9.4 g
- Protein: 13.4 g

20. BBQ Pork Chops

Basic Recipe

Preparation Time: 10 minutes

Cooking Time: 7 minutes

Servings: 4

Ingredients:

4 pork chops

For Rub:

- ½ teaspoon allspice
- ½ teaspoon dry mustard
- 1 teaspoon ground cumin
- 1 teaspoon garlic powder
- ½ teaspoon chili powder
- ½ teaspoon paprika
- 1 tablespoon brown sugar
- 1 teaspoon salt

Directions:

1. In a small bowl, mix together all rub ingredients and rub all over pork chops.
2. Arrange pork chops on air fryer tray and air fry at 400°F for 5.
3. Turn pork chops to the other side and air fry for 2 minutes more.
4. Serve and enjoy.

Nutrition:

- Calories: 273 kcal
- Fat: 20.2 g
- Carbs: 3.4 g
- Protein: 18.4 g

21. Simple Beef Sirloin Roast

Basic Recipe

Preparation Time: 10 minutes

Cooking Time: 50 minutes

Servings: 8

Ingredients:

- 2½ pounds sirloin roast
- Salt and ground black pepper, as required

Directions:

1. Season the roast well with salt and black pepper.
2. Through the roast, insert the rotisserie rod.
3. To secure the rod to the bird, place one rotisserie fork on each side of the rod.
4. Place the drip pan in the cooking chamber of the Air Fryer Oven.
5. Choose "Roast" and set the temperature to 350°F.
6. Press the "Start" button after selecting the timer for 50 minutes.
7. Press the red lever down and load the left side of the rod into the Vortex when the display says "Add Food."
8. Now, slide the rod's left side into the metal bar's groove to keep it from moving. Then close the door and press the "Rotate" button. When the cooking time is up, press the red lever to release the rod.
9. Remove the roast from the Vortex and set it aside for 10 minutes before slicing. Cut the roast into desired-sized slices with a sharp knife and serve.

Nutrition:

- Calories: 201 kcal
- Fat: 8.8 g
- Carbs: 0 g
- Protein: 28.9 g

22. Seasoned Beef Roast

Basic Recipe

Preparation Time: 10 minutes

Cooking Time: 45 minutes

Servings: 10

Ingredients:

- 3 pounds beef top roast
- 1 tablespoon olive oil
- 2 tablespoons Montreal steak seasoning

Directions:

1. Coat the roast with oil, then season thoroughly with the seasoning.
2. Tie the roast with kitchen twines to keep it compact. Place the roast on the baking sheet.
3. Place the drip pan in the cooking chamber of the Air Fryer Oven.
4. Choose "Air Fry" and set the temperature to 360°F. Press the "Start" button after setting the timer for 45 minutes.
5. Place the cooking tray in the center position when the display says "Add Food."
6. Do nothing when the display says "Turn Food."

- Remove the tray from the Vortex when the cooking time is up and set the roast on a platter for about 10 minutes before slicing. Cut the roast into desired-sized slices with a sharp knife and serve.

Nutrition:

- Calories: 269 kcal
- Fat: 9.9 g
- Carbs: 0 g
- Fiber: 0 g

23. Season and Salt-Cured Beef

Preparation Time: 15 minutes

Cooking Time: 3 hours

Servings: 4

Intermediate Recipe

Ingredients:

- 1½ pounds beef round, trimmed
- ½ cup Worcestershire sauce
- ½ cup low-sodium soy sauce
- 2 teaspoons honey
- 1 teaspoon liquid smoke
- 2 teaspoons onion powder
- ½ teaspoon red pepper flakes
- Ground black pepper, as required

Directions:

1. In a zip-top bag, place the beef and freeze for 1-2 hours to firm up.
2. Place the meat onto a cutting board and cut against the grain into 1/8-¼-inch strips.
3. In a large bowl, add the remaining ingredients and mix until well combined.
4. Add the steak slices and coat with the mixture generously.
5. Refrigerate to marinate for about 4-6 hours.
6. Remove the beef slices from the bowl, and with paper towels, pat dry them.
7. Divide the steak strips onto the cooking trays and arrange them in an even layer.
8. Select "Dehydrate" and then adjust the temperature to 160°F.
9. Set the timer for 3 hours and press the "Start."
10. When the display shows "Add Food" insert 1 tray in the top and center positions.
11. After 1½ hours, switch the position of cooking trays.
12. Meanwhile, add the remaining ingredients over medium heat in a small pan and cook for about 10 minutes, stirring occasionally.
13. When cooking time is complete, remove the trays from Vortex.

Nutrition:

- Calories: 372 kcal
- Fat: 10.7 g
- Carbs: 12 g
- Protein: 53.8 g

24. Sweet & Spicy Meatballs

Basic Recipe

Preparation Time: 20 minutes

Cooking Time: 30 minutes

Servings: 8

Ingredients:

For Meatballs:

- 2 pounds lean ground beef
- 2/3 cup quick-cooking oats
- ½ cup Ritz crackers, crushed
- 1 (5-ounce) can evaporated milk
- 2 large eggs, beaten lightly
- 1 teaspoon honey
- 1 tablespoon dried onion, minced
- 1 teaspoon garlic powder
- 1 teaspoon ground cumin
- Salt and ground black pepper, as required

For Sauce:

- 1/3 cup orange marmalade
- 1/3 cup honey
- 1/3 cup brown sugar
- 2 tablespoons cornstarch
- 2 tablespoons soy sauce
- 1-2 tablespoons hot sauce
- 1 tablespoon Worcestershire sauce

Directions:

1. To make the meatballs, combine all the ingredients in a large mixing basin and stir until well blended.
2. Form the mixture into 112-inch balls.
3. Place half of the meatballs in a single layer on a baking sheet.
4. Place the drip pan in the cooking chamber of the Air Fryer Oven.
5. Choose "Air Fry" and set the temperature to 380°F.
6. Press the "Start" button after setting the timer for 15 minutes.
7. Place the cooking tray in the center position when the display says "Add Food."
8. Turn the meatballs when the display says "Turn Food."
9. Remove the tray from the Vortex after the cooking time is finished.
10. Carry on with the remaining meatballs in the same manner.
11. Meanwhile, make the sauce by combining all the ingredients in a small saucepan and cooking over medium heat, constantly stirring until thickened.
12. Serve the meatballs with a sauce topping.

Nutrition:

- Calories: 411 kcal
- Fat: 11.1 g
- Calories: 411 kcal
- Fat: 11.1 g

Chapter 5 Fish

25. Salmon

Basic Recipe

Preparation Time: 5 minutes

Cooking Time: 12 minutes

Servings: 2

Ingredients:

- 2 salmon fillets, wild-caught, each about 1 ½ inch thick
- 1 teaspoon ground black pepper
- 2 teaspoons paprika
- 1 teaspoon salt
- 2 teaspoons olive oil

Directions:

1. Switch on the air fryer, insert fryer basket, grease it with olive oil, then shut with its lid, set the fryer at 390°F, and preheat for 5 minutes. Meanwhile, rub each salmon fillet with oil and then season with black pepper, paprika, and salt.
2. Open the fryer, add seasoned salmon in it, close with its lid and cook for 7 minutes until nicely golden and cooked, flipping the fillets halfway through the frying. When the air fryer beeps, open its lid, transfer salmon onto a serving plate and serve.

Nutrition:

- Calories: 288 kcal
- Carbs: 1.4 g
- Fat: 18.9 g
- Protein: 28.3 g

26. Parmesan Shrimp

Basic Recipe

Preparation Time: 10 minutes

Cooking Time: 10 minutes

Servings: 6

Ingredients:

- 2 pounds jumbo shrimp, wild-caught, peeled, deveined
- 2 tablespoons minced garlic
- 1 teaspoon onion powder
- 1 teaspoon basil
- 1 teaspoon ground black pepper
- 1/2 teaspoon dried oregano
- 2 tablespoons olive oil
- 2/3 cup grated parmesan cheese, reduced Fat: g
- 2 tablespoons lemon juice

Directions:

1. Switch on the air fryer, insert fryer basket, grease it with olive oil, then shut with its lid, set the fryer at 350°F, and preheat for 5 minutes
2. Meanwhile, place cheese in a bowl, add remaining ingredients except for shrimps and lemon juice and stir until combined.
3. Add shrimps and then toss until well coated.
4. Open the fryer, add shrimps in it, spray oil over them, close with its lid and cook for 10 minutes until nicely golden and crispy, shaking halfway through the frying. When the air fryer beeps, open its lid, transfer chicken onto a serving plate, drizzle with lemon juice and serve.

Nutrition:

- Calories: 307 kcal
- Carbs: 12 g
- Fat: 16.4 g
- Protein: 27.6 g

27. Fish Sticks

Basic Recipe

Preparation Time: 5 minutes

Cooking Time: 15 minutes

Servings: 4

Ingredients:

- 1-pound cod, wild-caught
- ½ teaspoon ground black pepper
- 3/4 teaspoon Cajun seasoning
- 1 teaspoon salt
- 1 1/2 cups pork rind
- 1/4 cup mayonnaise, reduced Fat: g
- 2 tablespoons water
- 2 tablespoons Dijon mustard

Directions:

1. Switch on the air fryer, insert fryer basket, grease it with olive oil, then shut with its lid, set the fryer at 400°F, and preheat for 5 minutes
2. Meanwhile, place mayonnaise in a bowl and then whisk in water and mustard until blended.
3. Place pork rinds in a shallow dish, add Cajun seasoning, black pepper, and salt and stir until mixed.
4. Cut the cod into 1 by 2 inches pieces, then dip into mayonnaise mixture and then coat with pork rind mixture.
5. Open the fryer; add fish sticks in it, spray with oil, close with its lid and cook for 10 minutes until nicely golden and crispy, flipping the sticks halfway through the frying.
6. When the air fryer beeps, open its lid, transfer fish sticks onto a serving plate and serve.

Nutrition:

- Calories: 263 kcal
- Carbs: 1 g
- Fat: 16 g
- Protein: 26.4 g

28. Shrimp with Lemon and Chile

Basic Recipe

Preparation Time: 5 minutes

Cooking Time: 12 minutes

Servings: 2

Ingredients:

- 1-pound shrimp, wild-caught, peeled, deveined
- 1 lemon, sliced
- 1 small red chili pepper, sliced
- ½ teaspoon ground black pepper
- 1/2 teaspoon garlic powder
- 1 teaspoon salt
- 1 tablespoon olive oil

Directions:

1. Switch on the air fryer, insert fryer basket, grease it with olive oil, then shut with its lid, set the fryer at 400°F, and preheat for 5 minutes
2. Meanwhile, place shrimps in a bowl, add garlic, salt, black pepper, oil, and lemon slices, and toss until combined. Open the fryer, add shrimps and lemon in it, close with its lid and cook for 5 minutes, shaking halfway through the frying. Then add chili slices, shake the basket until mixed and continue cooking for 2 minutes or until shrimps are opaque and crispy. When the air fryer beeps, open its lid, transfer shrimps and lemon slices onto a serving plate, and serve.

29. Tilapia

Basic Recipe

Preparation Time: 5 minutes

Cooking Time: 12 minutes

Servings: 2

- 2 tilapia fillets, wild-caught,
- 1 ½ inch thick
- 1 teaspoon old bay seasoning
- ¾ teaspoon lemon pepper seasoning
- ½ teaspoon salt

Ingredients:

Directions:

1. Switch on the air fryer, insert fryer basket, grease it with olive oil, then shut with its lid, set the fryer at 400°F, and preheat for 5 minutes

2. Meanwhile, spray tilapia fillets with oil and then season with salt, lemon pepper, and old bay seasoning until evenly coated. Open the fryer, add tilapia in it, close with its lid and cook for 7 minutes until nicely golden and cooked, turning the fillets halfway through the frying. When the air fryer beeps, open its lid, transfer tilapia fillets onto a serving plate and serve.

Nutrition:

- Calories: 36 kcal
- Carbs: 0 g
- Fat: 0.75 g
- Protein: 7.4 g

30. Tomato Basil Scallops

Basic Recipe

Preparation Time: 5 minutes

Cooking Time: 15 minutes

Servings: 2

Ingredients:

- 8 jumbo sea scallops, wild-caught
- 1 tablespoon tomato paste
- 12 ounces frozen spinach, thawed and dry out
- 1 tablespoon chopped fresh basil
- 1 teaspoon ground black pepper
- 1 teaspoon minced garlic
- 1 teaspoon salt
- 3/4 cup heavy whipping cream, reduced fat

Directions:

1. Switch on the air fryer, insert fryer basket, grease it with olive oil, then shut with its lid, set the fryer at 350°F, and preheat for 5 minutes
2. Meanwhile, take a 7 inches baking pan, grease it with oil, and place spinach in it in an even layer.
3. Spray the scallops with oil, sprinkle with ½ teaspoon each of salt and black pepper, and then place scallops over the spinach.
4. Place tomato paste in a bowl, whisk in cream, basil, garlic, and remaining salt and black pepper until smooth, and then pour over the scallops.
5. Open the fryer, place the pan in it, close with its lid, and cook for 10 minutes until thoroughly cooked and sauce is hot.
6. Serve straight away.

Nutrition:

- Calories: 359 kcal
- Carbs: 6 g
- Fat: 33 g
- Protein: 9 g

31. Shrimp Scampi

Basic Recipe

Preparation Time: 5 minutes

Cooking Time: 12 minutes

Servings: 4

Ingredients:

- 1-pound shrimp, peeled, deveined
- 1 tablespoon minced garlic
- 1 tablespoon minced basil
- 1 tablespoon lemon juice
- 1 teaspoon dried chives
- 1 teaspoon dried basil
- 2 teaspoons red pepper flakes
- 4 tablespoons butter, unsalted
- 2 tablespoons chicken stock

Directions:

1. Switch on the air fryer, insert fryer pan, grease it with olive oil, then shut with its lid, set the fryer at 330°F, and preheat for 5 minutes
2. Add butter in it along with red pepper and garlic and cook for 2 minutes or until the butter has melted.
3. Then add remaining ingredients in the pan, stir until mixed and continue cooking for 5 minutes until shrimps have cooked, stirring halfway through.
4. When done, remove the pan from the air fryer, stir the shrimp scampi, let it rest for 1 minute and then stir again.
5. Garnish shrimps with basil leaves and serve.

Nutrition:

- Calories: 221 kcal
- Carbs: 1 g
- Fat: 13 g
- Protein: 23 g

32. Salmon Cakes

Basic Recipe

Preparation Time: 5 minutes

Cooking Time: 12 minutes

Servings: 2

Ingredients:

- ¼ teaspoon ground black pepper
- 2 teaspoons Dijon mustard
- 2 tablespoons chopped fresh dill
- 2 tablespoons mayonnaise, reduced Fat:
- 1 egg, pastured
- 2 lemon wedges
- ½ cup almond flour
- 15 ounces cooked pink salmon

Directions:

1. Switch on the air fryer, insert fryer basket, grease it with olive oil, then shut with its lid, set the fryer at 400°F, and preheat for 5 minutes
2. Meanwhile, place all the ingredients in a bowl, except for lemon wedges, stir until combined and then shape into four patties, each about 4-inches. Open the fryer, add salmon patties in it, spray oil over them, close with its lid and cook for 12 minutes until nicely golden and crispy, flipping the patties halfway through the frying.
3. When the air fryer beeps, open its lid, transfer salmon patties onto a serving plate and serve.

Nutrition:

- Calories: 517 kcal
- Carbs: 15 g
- Fat: 27 g
- Protein: 52 g

33. Cilantro Lime Shrimps

Basic Recipe

Preparation Time: 25 minutes

Cooking Time: 21 minutes

Servings: 4

Ingredients:

- 1/2-pound shrimp, peeled, deveined
- 1/2 teaspoon minced garlic
- 1 tablespoon chopped cilantro
- 1/2 teaspoon paprika
- ¾ teaspoon salt
- 1/2 teaspoon ground cumin
- 2 tablespoons lemon juice

Directions:

1. Take 6 wooden skewers and let them soak in warm water for 20 minutes
2. Meanwhile, switch on the air fryer, insert the fryer basket, grease it with olive oil, then shut with its lid, set the fryer at 350°F, and let preheat.
3. Whisk together lemon juice, paprika, salt, cumin, and garlic in a large bowl, then add shrimps and toss until well coated.
4. Dry out the skewers and then thread shrimps in them.
5. Open the fryer, add shrimps in it in a single layer, spray oil over them, close with its lid and cook for 8 minutes until nicely golden and cooked, turning the skewers halfway through the frying.
6. When the air fryer beeps, open its lid, transfer shrimps onto a serving plate, and keep them warm.
7. Cook remaining shrimp skewers in the same manner and serve.

Nutrition:

- Calories: 59 kcal
- Carbs: 0.3 g
- Fat: 1.5 g
- Protein: 11 g

34. Cajun Style Shrimp

Basic Recipe

Preparation Time: 3 minutes

Cooking Time: 10 minutes

Servings: 2

Ingredients:

- 6 g salt
- 2 g smoked paprika
- 2 g garlic powder
- 2 g Italian seasoning
- 2 g chili powder
- 1 g onion powder
- 1 g cayenne pepper
- 1 g black pepper
- 1 g dried thyme
- 454 g large shrimp, peeled and unveiled
- 30 ml of olive oil
- Lime wedges, to serve

Directions:

1. Select Preheat, in the air fryer, set the temperature to 190°C, and press Start/Pause. Combine all seasonings in a large bowl. Set aside
2. Mix the shrimp with olive oil until they are evenly coated. Sprinkle the dressing mixture over the shrimp and stir until well coated. Place the shrimp in the preheated air fryer.
3. Select shrimp; then, set the time to 5 minutes, and press Start/Pause. Shake the baskets in the middle of cooking. Serve with pieces of lime.

Nutrition:

- Calories: 126 kcal
- Fat: 6 g
- Carbs: 2 g
- Protein: 33 g

35. Crab Cakes

Intermediate Recipe

Preparation Time: 10 minutes

Cooking Time: 40 minutes

Servings: 2

Ingredients:

For Crab Cakes:

- 1 large egg, beaten
- 17 g of mayonnaise
- 11 g Dijon mustard
- 5 ml Worcestershire sauce
- 2 g Old Bay seasoning
- 2 g salt
- A white pepper pinch
- A cayenne pinch
- 26 g celery, finely diced
- 45 g red pepper, finely diced
- 8 g fresh parsley, finely chopped
- 227 g crab meat
- 28 g breadcrumbs
- Nonstick Spray Oil

Remodeled:

- 55 g mayonnaise
- 15 g capers washed and dry outed
- 5 g sweet pickles, chopped
- 5 g red onion, finely chopped
- 8 ml lemon juice
- 8 g Dijon mustard
- Salt and pepper to taste

Directions:

1. Mix the ingredients of remodeled until everything is well incorporated. Set aside
2. Beat the egg, mayonnaise, mustard, Worcestershire sauce, Old Bay seasoning, salt, white pepper, cayenne pepper, celery, pepper, and parsley.
3. Gently stir the crab meat in the egg mixture and stir it until well mixed. Sprinkle the breadcrumbs over the crab mixture and fold them gently until the breadcrumbs cover every corner.
4. Shape the crab mixture into 4 cakes and chill in the fridge for 30 minutes. Select Preheat in the air fryer and press Start/Pause.
5. Place a sheet of baking paper in the basket of the preheated air fryer. Sprinkle the crab cakes with cooking spray and place them gently on the paper. Cook the crab cakes at 205°C for 8 minutes until golden brown.
6. Flip crab cakes during cooking. Serve with remodeled.

Nutrition:

- Calories: 110 kcal
- Fat: 6.5 g
- Carbs: 5.5 g
- Protein: 7 g

36. Tuna Pie

Basic Recipe

Preparation Time: 10 minutes

Cooking Time: 30 minutes

Serving: 4

Ingredients:

- 2 hard-boiled eggs
- 2 tuna cans
- 200 ml fried tomato
- 1 sheet broken dough

Directions:

1. Cut the eggs into small pieces and mix with the tuna and tomato.
2. Spread the sheet of broken dough and cut it into two equal squares.
3. Put the mixture of tuna, eggs, and tomato on one of the squares.
4. Cover with the other, join at the ends and decorate with leftover little pieces.
5. Preheat the air fryer for a few minutes at 180°C.
6. Enter in the air fryer basket and set the timer for 15 minutes at 180°C

Nutrition:

- Calories: 244 kcal
- Fat: 13.67 g
- Carbs: 21.06 g
- Protein: 8.72 g

Chapter 6 Vegan

37. Eggplant with Grated Cheddar

Basic Recipe

Preparation Time: 15 minutes

Cooking Time: 10 minutes

Servings: 10

Ingredients:

- 2 Eggplants
- 1 teaspoon minced garlic
- 1 teaspoon olive oil
- 4 oz Cheddar cheese, grated
- ½ teaspoon ground black pepper

Directions:

1. Wash the eggplants carefully and slice them.
2. Rub the slices with minced garlic, salt, and ground black pepper.
3. Leave the slices for 5 minutes to marinade.
4. Preheat the air fryer to 400°F.
5. Place the eggplant circles in the air fryer rack and cook them for 6 minutes
6. Then turn them overcook for 5 minutes more.
7. Sprinkle the eggplants with the grated cheese and cook for 30 seconds.
8. Serve hot.

Nutrition:

- Calories: 97 kcal
- Fat: 6.2 g
- Carbs: 7.7 g
- Protein: 5.2 g

38. Coriander Garlic Bulbs

Basic Recipe

Preparation Time: 10 minutes

Cooking Time: 10 minutes

Servings: 18

Ingredients:

- 1-pound garlic heads
- 2 tablespoons olive oil
- 1 teaspoon dried oregano
- 1 teaspoon dried basil
- 1 teaspoon ground coriander
- ¼ teaspoon ground ginger

Directions:

1. Cut the ends of the garlic bulb
2. Place each bulb on foil.
3. Coat them with olive oil, dried oregano, dried basil, ground coriander, and ground ginger.
4. Preheat the air fryer to 400°F.
5. Wrap the garlic in foil and place it in the air fryer.
6. Cook for 10 minutes until soft.
7. Let them cool for at least 10 minutes before serving.

Nutrition:

- Calories: 57 kcal
- Fat: 1.4 g
- Carbs: 8.2 g
- Protein: 1.3 g

39. Parmesan Sticks

Basic Recipe

Preparation Time: 10 minutes

Cooking Time: 10 minutes

Servings: 3

Ingredients:

- 2 Oz Parmesan
- 1 egg
- ½ cup heavy cream
- 2 Tablespoons almond flour
- ¼ teaspoon ground black pepper

Directions:

1. Crack the egg in a bowl and whisk.
2. Add the heavy cream and almond flour.
3. Sprinkle the mixture with ground black pepper.
4. Whisk carefully or use a hand mixer.
5. Cut the cheese into thick short sticks
6. Dip the sticks in the heavy cream mixture.
7. Place the cheese sticks in freezer bags and freeze them.
8. Preheat the air fryer to 400°F.
9. Place the cheese sticks in the air fryer rack.
10. Cook for 8 minutes

Nutrition:

- Calories: 389 kcal
- Fat: 29.5 g
- Carbs: 5.5 g
- Protein: 28.6 g

40. Creamy Snow Peas

Basic Recipe

Preparation Time: 10 minutes

Cooking Time: 5 minutes

Servings: 5

Ingredients:

- ½ cup heavy cream
- 1 teaspoon butter
- 1 teaspoon salt
- 1 teaspoon paprika
- 1-pound snow peas
- ¼ teaspoon nutmeg

Directions:

1. Preheat the air fryer to 400°F.
2. Wash the snow peas carefully and place them in the air fryer basket tray.
3. Then sprinkle the snow peas with butter, salt, paprika, nutmeg, and heavy cream.
4. Cook the snow peas for 5 minutes
5. When the time is over—shake the snow peas gently and transfer them to the serving plates.
6. Enjoy!

Nutrition:

- Calories: 98 kcal
- Fat: 5.9 g
- Carbs: 6.9 g
- Protein: 3.5 g

41. Sesame Okra

Basic Recipe

Preparation Time: 10 minutes

Cooking Time: 4 minutes

Servings: 4

- 1 tablespoon sesame oil
- 1 teaspoon sesame seed
- 5 Oz okra
- ½ teaspoon salt
- 1 egg

Ingredients:

Directions:

1. Wash the okra and chop it roughly.
2. Crack the egg into a bowl and whisk it.
3. Add the chopped okra to the whisked egg.
4. Sprinkle with the sesame seeds and salt.
5. Preheat the air fryer to 400°F.
6. Mix the okra mixture carefully.
7. Place the mixture in the air fryer basket.
8. Drizzle with olive oil.
9. Cook the okra for 4 minutes
10. Stir and serve.

Nutrition:

- Calories: 81 kcal
- Fat: 5 g
- Carbs: 6.1 g
- Protein: 3 g

42. Fennel Oregano Wedges

Basic Recipe

Preparation Time: 15 minutes

Cooking Time: 6 minutes

Servings: 4

Ingredients:

- 1 teaspoon stevia extract
- ½ teaspoon fresh thyme
- ½ teaspoon salt
- 1 teaspoon olive oil
- 14 oz fennel
- 1 teaspoon butter
- 1 teaspoon dried oregano
- ½ teaspoon chili flakes

Directions:

1. Slice the fennel into wedges. Melt the butter. Combine the butter, olive oil, dried oregano, and chili flakes in a bowl.
2. Combine well.
3. Add salt, fresh thyme, and stevia extract. Whisk

gently.

4. Brush the fennel wedges with the mixture. Preheat the air fryer to 370°F.
5. Place the fennel wedges in the air fryer rack.
6. Cook the fennel wedges for 3 minutes on each side.

Nutrition:

- Calories: 41 kcal
- Fat: 1.9 g
- Carbs: 6.1 g
- Protein: 1 g

43. Parsley Kohlrabi Fritters

Basic Recipe

Preparation Time: 10 minutes

Cooking Time: 7 minutes

Servings: 4

Ingredients:

- 5 Oz kohlrabi
- 1 egg
- 1 tablespoon almond flour
- ½ teaspoon salt
- 1 teaspoon olive oil
- 1 teaspoon ground black pepper
- 1 tablespoon dried parsley
- ¼ teaspoon chili pepper

Directions:

1. Peel the kohlrabi and grate it. Combine the grated kohlrabi with salt, ground black pepper, dried parsley, and chili pepper.
2. Crack the egg into the mixture and whisk it. Make medium fritters from the mixture.
3. Preheat the air fryer to 380°F. Grease the air fryer basket tray with olive oil and place the fritters inside. Cook the fritters for 4 minutes. Turn the fritters and cook for 3 minutes more. Allow cooling slightly before serving.

Nutrition:

- Calories: 66 kcal
- Fat: 4.7 g
- Carbs: 4.4 g
- Protein: 3.2 g

44. Chives Bamboo Shoots

Basic Recipe

Preparation Time: 10 minutes

Cooking Time: 4 minutes

Servings: 2

Ingredients:

- 4 Oz bamboo shoots
- garlic cloves, sliced
- 2 1 tablespoon olive oil
- ½ teaspoon chili flakes
- 1 tablespoon chives
- ½ teaspoon salt
- 2ctablespoons fish stock

Directions:

1. Preheat the air fryer to 400°F. Cut the bamboo shoots into strips.

2. Combine the sliced garlic cloves, olive oil, chili flakes, salt, and fish stock in the air fryer basket tray. Cook for 1 minute.
3. Stir the mixture gently. Add the bamboo strips and chives.
4. Stir the dish carefully and cook for 3 minutes more.
5. Stir again before serving.

Nutrition:

- Calories: 100 kcal
- Fat: 7.6 g
- Carbs: 7 g
- Protein: 3.7 g

45. Summer Eggplant & Zucchini

Basic Recipe

Preparation Time: 15 minutes

Cooking Time: 15 minutes

Servings: 8

Ingredients:

- 1 eggplant
- 1 tomato
- 1 zucchini
- 5 Oz chive stems
- 2 tbsp green peppers
- 1 teaspoon paprika
- 1 tablespoon olive oil
- ½ teaspoon ground nutmeg
- ½ teaspoon ground thyme
- 1 teaspoon salt

Directions:

1. Preheat the air fryer to 390°F.
2. Wash the eggplant, tomato, and zucchini carefully.
3. Chop all the vegetables roughly.
4. Place the chopped vegetables in the air fryer basket tray.
5. Coat the vegetables with paprika, olive oil, ground nutmeg, ground thyme, and salt.
6. Stir the vegetables using two spatulas.
7. Cut the green peppers into squares.
8. Add the squares into the vegetable mixture. Stir gently.
9. Cook for 15 minutes, stirring after 10 minutes, then serve.

Nutrition:

- Calories: 48 kcal
- Fat: 2.1 g
- Fiber 3.3 g
- Carbs: 7.4 g
- Protein: 1.4 g

46. Zucchini Hassel back

Basic Recipe

Preparation Time: 15 minutes

Cooking Time: 12 minutes

Servings: 2

Ingredients:

- 1 zucchini
- 4 Oz Cheddar, sliced
- ½ teaspoon salt
- ½ teaspoon dried oregano
- ½ teaspoon ground coriander
- ½ teaspoon paprika
- 2 tablespoons heavy cream
- 1 teaspoon olive oil
- ¼ teaspoon minced garlic

Directions:

1. Cut the zucchini into a Hassel back shape.
2. Then fill the zucchini with the sliced cheese.
3. Coat the zucchini Hassel back with salt, dried oregano, ground coriander, paprika, minced garlic, olive oil, and heavy cream.
4. Preheat the air fryer to 400°F.
5. Wrap the zucchini Hassel back in foil and place it in the preheated air fryer.
6. Cook for 12 minutes
7. When the zucchini is cooked, remove it from the foil and cut it into 2 pieces.

Nutrition:

- Calories: 215 kcal
- Fat: 14.9 g
- Carbs: 5.7 g
- Protein: 15.6 g

47. Butternut Squash Hash

Basic Recipe

Preparation Time: 10 minutes

Cooking Time: 14 minutes

Servings: 4

Ingredients:

- 1 cup chicken stock
- 4 Oz butternut squash
- 1 teaspoon salt
- 1 tablespoon butter
- 1 teaspoon dried dill

- ¼ teaspoon paprika

Directions:

1. Peel the butternut squash and chop it.
2. Preheat the air fryer to 370°F.
3. Pour the chicken stock into the air fryer basket tray.
4. Add salt, chopped butternut squash, butter, dried dill, and paprika.
5. Stir gently.
6. Cook for 14 minutes.
7. Transfer to a bowl.
8. Use a fork to mash.
9. Serve immediately.

Nutrition:

- Calories: 61 kcal
- Fat: 3.3 g
- Carbs: 6.2 g
- Protein: 0.9 g

48. Butter Mushrooms with Chives

Basic Recipe

Preparation Time: 10 minutes

Cooking Time: 10 minutes

Servings: 2

Ingredients:

- 1 cup white mushrooms
- 4 Oz chive stems
- 1 tablespoon butter
- 1 teaspoon olive oil
- 1 teaspoon dried rosemary
- 1/3 teaspoon salt
- ¼ teaspoon ground nutmeg

Directions:

1. Preheat the air fryer to 400°F.
2. Pour the olive oil and butter into the air fryer basket tray.
3. Add dried rosemary, salt, and ground nutmeg.
4. Stir gently.
5. Dice the chives.
6. Add the diced chives to the air fryer basket tray.
7. Cook for 5 minutes
8. Meanwhile, chop the white mushrooms.
9. Add the mushrooms.
10. Stir the mixture and cook it for a further 5 minutes at the same temperature.
11. Stir, then serve.

Nutrition:

- Calories: 104 kcal
- Fat: 8.4 g
- Carbs: 6.8 g
- Protein: 1.8 g

Chapter 7 Vegetarian

49. Tangy Mushroom Pizza

Intermediate Recipe

Preparation time: 8–10 min.

Cooking Time: 8 min.

Servings: 3–4

Ingredients:

- 3 tablespoons olive oil
- 3 cleaned portabella mushroom caps, scooped
- 3 tablespoons tomato sauce
- 12 slices pepperoni
- 3 tablespoons mozzarella, shredded
- 1 pinch salt
- 1 pinch dried Italian seasoning

Directions:

1. Place your air fryer on a flat kitchen surface; plug it and turn it on. Set temperature to 330°F and let it preheat for 4-5 minutes.
2. Take out the air-frying basket and gently coat it using cooking oil or spray.
3. Now take the mushrooms and spread oil over them. On their inner side, add Italian seasoning and salt. Top with the tomato sauce and cheese.
4. Add the mushrooms to the basket. Push the air-frying basket in the air fryer. Cook for 2 minutes.
5. Slide out the basket; add the slices of pepperoni and cook for 4-5 more minutes. Top with red pepper flakes and more cheese (optional).

Nutrition:

- Calories: 153 kcal
- Fat: 14 g
- Carbs: 5.1 g
- Fiber: 1 g
- Protein: 5.4 g

50. Classic Zucchini Polenta

Intermediate Recipe

Preparation time: 10-15 min.

Cooking Time: 40 min.

Servings: 5-6

Ingredients:

- 1/2-pound zucchini, cut into bite-sized chunks
- 1/2-pound potatoes, make bite-sized chunks
- 1/2 teaspoon ground black pepper
- 1/2 teaspoon dried dill weed
- 1 tablespoon olive oil
- 1 cup onions, chopped
- 2 cloves garlic, finely minced
- 1 teaspoon paprika
- 1/2 teaspoon salt
- 14 ounces pre-cooked polenta tube, make slices
- 1/4 cup cheddar cheese, shaved

Directions:

1. Place your air fryer on a flat kitchen surface; plug it and turn it on. Set temperature to 400°F and let it preheat for 4-5 minutes.
2. Add the veggies to the basket. Add the olive oil, paprika, salt, pepper, and dill. Combine well.
3. Push the air-frying basket in the air fryer. Cook for 6 minutes.
4. Slide out the basket, shake, and cook for 6 more minutes. Transfer to a serving plate.
5. In the basket, add some cooking oil and polenta. Cook for 20-25 minutes.
6. Slide out the basket; turn the polenta and cook for 10 more minutes. Top each polenta slice with roasted vegetables and cheese.

Nutrition:

- Calories: 135 kcal
- Fat: 4 g
- Carbs: 20 g
- Fiber: 2 g
- Protein: 4 g

51. Risotto Croquettes

Intermediate Recipe

Preparation time: 10-15 min.

Cooking Time: 15 min.

Servings: 4

Ingredients:

- Sea salt as needed
- 1/4 teaspoon ground black pepper
- 1 tablespoon Colby cheese, grated
- 1 egg, beaten
- 1 cup breadcrumbs
- 1/2 teaspoon dried dill weed
- 1 teaspoon paprika
- 2 garlic cloves, peeled and minced
- 1/2 cup mushrooms, chopped
- 6 ounces cooked rice
- 1 tablespoon rice bran oil
- 1 onion, chopped

Directions:

1. Take a medium-sized saucepan and add in the oil, garlic, and onion; heat the pan on medium heat until turn soft.
2. Add in the mushrooms and cook until the liquid gets evaporated. Cool down the mixture.
3. Add the cooked rice, salt, black pepper, dill, and paprika. Combine well. Add the cheese and mix again. Make risotto balls from the mixture.
4. Dip in the beaten egg; then, roll them in the breadcrumbs.
5. Place your air fryer on a flat kitchen surface; plug it and turn it on. Set temperature to 390°F and let it preheat for 4-5 minutes.
6. Take out the air-frying basket and gently coat it using cooking oil or spray.
7. Add the balls to the basket. Push the air-frying basket in the air fryer. Cook for 7 minutes.
8. Slide out the basket; cook for 2 more minutes, if needed. Serve warm with marinara sauce.

Nutrition:

- Calories: 319 kcal
- Fat: 6.7 g
- Carbs: 52.1 g
- Fiber: 3.5 g
- Protein: 9 g

52. Spiced Bean Meal

Intermediate Recipe

Preparation time: 8-10 min.

Cooking Time: 8 min.

Servings: 4

Ingredients:

- 1/2 teaspoon black pepper
- 1 teaspoon sea salt flakes
- 1/2 cup all-purpose flour
- 1 teaspoon smoky chipotle powder
- 2 eggs, beaten
- 10 ounces wax beans
- 1/2 cup saltines, crushed

Directions:

1. In a bowl of medium size, thoroughly mix the flour, chipotle powder, black pepper, and salt. In a bowl of medium size, thoroughly whisk the eggs.
2. Add the crushed saltines to another bowl. Coat the beans with the flour mixture; then, coat with the beaten egg. Lastly, roll them over the crushed saltines.
3. Top the beans with a non-stick cooking spray.
4. Place your air fryer on a flat kitchen surface; plug it and turn it on. Set temperature to 360°F and let it preheat for 4-5 minutes.
5. Add the mixture to the basket. Push the air-frying basket in the air fryer. Cook for 4 minutes.
6. Slide out the basket; shake, and cook for 3 more minutes. Serve warm!

Nutrition:

- Calories: 134 kcal
- Fat: 2.9 g
- Carbs: 21 g
- Fiber: 2.3 g
- Protein: 6.4 g

53. Mozzarella Radish Salad

Intermediate Recipe

Preparation time: 8-10 min.

Cooking Time: 30 min.

Servings: 4

Ingredients:

- 1 ½ pounds radishes, trimmed and halved
- 2 tablespoons olive oil
- Pepper and salt, as needed

For the Salad:

- 1 teaspoon olive oil
- 1 tablespoon balsamic vinegar
- ½ pound mozzarella, sliced
- 1 teaspoon honey
- Pepper and salt, as needed

Directions:

1. In a bowl of medium size, thoroughly mix the radishes, salt, black pepper, and oil.
2. Place your air fryer on a flat kitchen surface; plug it and turn it on. Set temperature to 350°F and let it preheat for 4-5 minutes.
3. Add the mixture to the basket. Push the air-frying basket in the air fryer. Cook for 3 minutes.
4. In a bowl of medium size, thoroughly mix the fried radish and cheese.
5. In a bowl of small size, thoroughly mix the other ingredients and serve over the salad!

Nutrition:

- Calories: 363 kcal
- Fat: 29 g
- Carbs: 4 g
- Fiber: 0 g
- Protein: 2 g

54. Buffalo Cauliflower

Intermediate Recipe

Preparation time: 10 minutes

Cooking Time: 25 Minutes

- 2-3 tablespoons hot sauce
- 1½ teaspoons pure maple syrup
- 2 teaspoons avocado oil
- 2-3 tablespoons nutritional yeast
- ¼ teaspoon sea salt
- 1 tablespoon cornstarch
- 6 cups ½ "cauliflower florets

Ingredients:

Directions:

1. Place the air fryer to 360°F.
2. Add the hot sauce, maple syrup, avocado oil, nutritional yeast, sea salt, and cornstarch to a large-size bowl. Whisk well to incorporate fully.
3. Add the cauliflower florets and toss to coat well and evenly.
4. Add approximately half of the florets to your air fryer basket.
5. Cook in the air fryer for 12-14 minutes, shaking the basket halfway through cooking until the florets are your preferred consistency.
6. Repeat the process with the remaining cauliflower florets for 8-10 minutes.
7. Serve and enjoy.

Nutrition:

- Calories: 187 kcal
- Fat: 7 g
- Protein: 15 g
- Sugar: 2 g

55. Buttermilk Fried Mushrooms

Intermediate Recipe

Preparation time: 5 minutes

Cooking Time: 45 Minutes

Servings: 2

Ingredients:

- 2 cups cleaned oyster mushrooms
- 1 cup buttermilk
- 1½ cups all-purpose flour
- 1 teaspoon salt
- 1 teaspoon black pepper
- 1 teaspoon garlic powder
- 1 teaspoon onion powder
- 1 teaspoon smoked paprika
- 1 teaspoon cumin
- 1 tablespoon oil

Directions:

1. Preheat your air fryer to 375°F.
2. Toss the mushrooms with the buttermilk and set them aside to marinate for 15 minutes.
3. In a second larger bowl, combine the flour with the salt, pepper, garlic powder, onion powder, smoked paprika, cumin, and oil.
4. Take the mushrooms out of the buttermilk, setting the buttermilk to one side.
5. Dip each mushroom in the flour mixture, shaking off any excess flour. Dip the mushrooms once again in the buttermilk, then once again in the flour.
6. Liberally grease the bottom of the air fryer pan.
7. In a single layer, allowing space between the mushrooms, add the mushrooms to the pan. Cook for 5 minutes before brushing them all over with a drop of oil.
8. Continue to cook for an additional 5-10 minutes, until crisp and golden.

Nutrition:

- Calories: 602 kcal
- Fat: 8 g
- Protein: 24 g

- Sugar: 11 g

56. Chinese Spring Rolls

Intermediate Recipe

Preparation time: 10 minutes

Cooking Time: 35 Minutes

Servings: 8

Ingredients:

- 2 tablespoons sesame oil
- ½ teaspoon minced garlic
- 2 cups shredded cabbage
- 1 cup matchstick-cut carrots
- ½ cup thinly sliced bamboo shoots
- 1 tablespoon freshly squeezed lime juice
- 2 teaspoons fish sauce
- 1 teaspoon soy sauce
- 8 square spring roll wrappers
- Water
- Spray oil

Directions:

1. Firstly, heat the oven to 390°F.
2. Over medium to high heat, heat sesame oil in a skillet or frying pan, add garlic, and cook for 30 seconds, until fragrant.
3. Add chopped cabbage, carrots, and bamboo shoots and cook for 4-5 minutes, until smooth.
4. Remove the pan from the heat and add the fresh lime juice followed by the fish sauce and soy sauce.
5. Fill each of the 8 spring wrappers with the vegetable mix. The filling should be just below the middle of the wrapper. Fold the bottom of the wrap over the filling to close it and press down. Fold both sides and roll hard. Use a drop of cold water to seal.
6. Repeat the process with the remaining ingredients until you have collected the 8 spring rolls.
7. Spray the fryer basket and springs with cooking spray.
8. In a single layer, and if you work in batches, if necessary, add springs to the basket. Fry the rolls with a spring for 5 minutes before turning them over and cook until golden, for an additional 5 minutes.
9. Remove from the fryer and serve.

Nutrition:

- Calories: 378 kcal
- Fat: 18 g
- Protein: 19 g
- Sugar: 4 g

57. Onion Pakoras

Intermediate Recipe

Preparation time: 10 minutes

Cooking Time: 45 Minutes

Servings: 2-3

Ingredients:

- 2 cups gram flour
- 2 cups peeled and sliced red onions
- ½ teaspoon carom seeds
- ¼ teaspoon asafetida
- ½ cup water
- 1-2 teaspoons oil for brushing
- Chopped coriander leaves to garnish
- Chopped green chilies, to garnish
- Salt, to taste
- 1 teaspoon red chili powder
- 1/3 Cup of rice flour

Directions:

1. Preheat the air fryer to 200°F for 8-10 minutes.
2. Meanwhile, in a bowl, combine the flour with the red onions, carom seeds, asafetida, red chili powder, and rice flour.
3. Slowly stir in the water to create a sticky, thick batter.
4. Add 1 teaspoon of oil to the batter and mix thoroughly.
5. When the air fryer is at the required temperature, place the batter on the Air Fryer mesh in small-size portions.
6. Lightly brush the pakoras with oil and air fry for 10 minutes.
7. Flip them over, brush with a little more oil, and air fry for 8 minutes.
8. Remove and serve hot.
9. Repeat the process with the remaining batter.

Nutrition:

- Calories: 506
- Fat: 2 g
- Protein: 22 g
- Sugar: 12 g

58. Onion Rings

Intermediate Recipe

Preparation time: 10 minutes

Cooking Time: 25 Minutes

Servings: 2

- 1/
- 1 cup panko breadcrumbs
- 2 tablespoons olive oil
- 1 large-size, peeled and sliced into "thick yellow sweet onion rings
- Spray oil

Ingredients:

- ½ cup all-purpose flour
- 1 teaspoon paprika
- 1 teaspoon salt
- ½ cup buttermilk
- 1 medium-size egg

Directions:

1. Gather 3 shallow dishes or bowls.
2. In the first dish, combine the flour with the paprika and ½ a teaspoon of salt.
3. In the second dish, combine the buttermilk with the egg.
4. Add a ¼ cup of the seasoned flour mixture to the buttermilk egg.
5. In the third dish or bowl, combine the breadcrumbs with ½ a teaspoon of salt and olive oil. Using a fork, mix until the oil is incorporated evenly.
6. Dredge the yellow onion rings first in the flour, second in the buttermilk mixture, and finally dredge them in the breadcrumb mixture.
7. In a single layer, add the coated onion rings to your air fryer basket. Try and leave space between the rings.
8. Cook the onion rings at 400°F until golden and crisp. This will take approximately 12-15 minutes. You will need to spray the rings with spray oil after approximately 6 minutes of air frying.
9. Transfer to a kitchen paper towel-lined plate to absorb any excess oil.
10. Serve and enjoy with your favorite dip or as an aside.

Nutrition:

- Calories: 442 kcal
- Fat: 9 g
- Protein: 28 g
- Sugar: 7 g

59. Lemon Broccoli

Intermediate Recipe

Preparation time: 10 minutes

Cooking Time: 10 to 14 minutes

Servings: 4

Ingredients:

- 1 large head fresh broccoli
- 2 teaspoons olive oil

1 tablespoon freshly squeezed lemon juice

1. Rinse the broccoli and pat dry. Cut off the florets and separate them.
2. Toss the broccoli, lemon juice, and olive oil until coated.
3. Roast the broccoli, in batches, at 380°F (193°C) for 10 to 14 minutes or until the broccoli is crisp-tender and slightly brown around the edges. Repeat with the remaining broccoli. Serve immediately.

Nutrition:

- Calories: 64 kcal
- Fat: 2 g
- Protein: 4 g
- Carbs: 10 g
- Fiber: 4 g
- Sugar: 3 g
- Sodium: 50 mg

60. Garlic Roasted Bell Peppers

Intermediate Recipe

Preparation time: 10 minutes

Cooking Time: 18 to 20 minutes

Servings: 4

Ingredients:

- 4 bell peppers, any colors, stemmed, seeded, membranes removed, and cut into fourths
- 1 teaspoon olive oil
- 4 garlic cloves, minced
- ½ teaspoon dried thyme

Nutrition:

- Calories: 37 kcal
- Fat: 1 g
- Protein: 1 g
- Carbs: 5 g
- Fiber: 2 g
- Sugar: 3 g
- Sodium: 21 mg

Chapter 8 Snacks

61. Air Fried Chicken Tenders

Basic Recipe

Preparation time: 10 minutes

Cooking Time: 10 minutes

Servings: 4

Ingredients:

- 1/8 cup flour
- Pepper and salt to taste
- Olive spray
- 1 egg white
- 12 oz, chicken breasts
- 1-¼ oz panko bread crumbs

Directions:

1. Trim off excess Fat: from your chicken breast. Cut into tenders. Season it with pepper and salt. Dip the tenders into flour and, after that, into egg whites and bread crumbs. Keep in the fryer basket. Apply olive spray and cook for 10 minutes at 350°F. Serve.

Nutrition:

- Calories: 399 kcal
- Carbs: 18 g
- Fat: 11 g
- Protein: 57 g

62. Parmesan Zucchini Chips

Basic Recipe

Preparation time: 15 minutes

Cooking Time: 10 minutes

Servings: 4

Ingredients:

- Salt to taste
- medium zucchinis
- cup grated Parmesan cheese

Directions:

1. Preheat the oven in Air Fryer mode at 110°F for 2 to 3 minutes.
2. Use a mandolin slicer to very finely slice the zucchinis, season with salt, and coat well with the Parmesan cheese.
3. In batches, arrange as lots of zucchini pieces as possible in a single layer on the cooking tray. When the device is ready, move the cooking tray onto the leading rack of the oven and close the oven. Set the timer to 7 minutes and press Start. Cook till the cheese melts while turning the midway. Transfer the chips to serving bowls to cool and make the remaining. Serve warm.

Nutrition:

- Calories: 107 kcal
- Fat: 6.99 g
- Carbs: 3.73 g
- Protein: 7.33 g

63. Cattle Ranch Garlic Pretzels

Basic Recipe

Preparation time: 10 minutes

Cooking Time: 15 minutes

Servings: 4

Ingredients:

- ½ teaspoon garlic powder
- 2 cups pretzels
- 1 ½ teaspoon ranch dressing mix
- 1 tablespoon melted butter

Directions:

1. Preheat the oven in Air Fryer mode at 270°F for 2 to 3 minutes.
2. In a medium bowl, blend all the ingredients up until well-integrated, pour into the rotisserie basket, and near to seal. Repair the basket onto the lever in the oven and close the oven.
3. Set the timer to 15 minutes, press Start, and cook until the pretzels are gently browned. After, open the oven, secure the basket utilizing the rotisserie lift and transfer the snack into serving bowls. Permit cooling and delight in.

Nutrition:

- Calories: 35 kcal
- Fat: 3.72 g
- Carbs: 0.4 g
- Protein: 0.12 g

64. Herby Sweet Potato Chips

Basic Recipe

Preparation time: 10 minutes

Cooking Time: 10 minutes

Servings: 4

Ingredients:

- 1 teaspoon dried mixed herbs
- 2 medium sweet potatoes, peeled
- 1 tablespoon olive oil

Directions:

1. Preheat the oven in Air Fry mode at 375°F for 2 to 3 minutes. On the other hand, utilize a mandolin slicer to thinly slice the sweet potatoes, transfer them to a medium bowl and blend well with the herbs and olive oil till well coated. In batches, organize as numerous sweet potato pieces as possible in a single layer on the cooking tray. When the device is ready, slide the cooking tray onto the top rack of the oven and close the oven. Set the timer to 7 minutes and press Start. Cook till the sweet potatoes are crispy while turning midway. Transfer the chips to serving bowls when prepared and make the remaining in the same manner. Delight in.

Nutrition:

- Calories: 87 kcal
- Fat: 3.48 g
- Carbs: 13.38 g
- Protein: 1.03 g

65. Cumin Tortilla Chips with Guacamole

Basic Recipe

Preparation time: 5 minutes

Cooking Time: 15 minutes

Servings: 4

Ingredients:

- 2 tablespoon olive oil
- 12 corn tortillas
- 1 tablespoon paprika powder
- 1 tablespoon cumin powder

For the tortilla chips:

- Salt and black pepper to taste

For the guacamole:

- 1 little company tomato, sliced
- A pinch dried parsley
- 1 big avocado, pitted and peeled

Directions:

1. Preheat the oven in Air Fry mode at 375°F for 2 to 3 minutes in a medium bowl, mix all the ingredients for the tortilla chips well and put the mix into the rotisserie basket. Close to seal. Fix the basket onto the lever in the oven and close the oven. Set the timer to 15 minutes, press Start, and cook until the tortillas are golden brown.
2. After, open the oven, take out the basket using the rotisserie lift and transfer the chips to serving bowls. Meanwhile, as the chips are cooked, mash the avocados in a little bowl and blend with the tomato and parsley until well combined.
3. Serve the tortilla chips with guacamole.

Nutrition:

- Calories: 159 kcal
- Fat: 14.74 g
- Carbs: 7.82 g
- Protein: 1.94 g

66. Oven-Dried Strawberries

Basic Recipe

Preparation time: 10 minutes

Cooking Time: 10 minutes

Servings: 4

Ingredients:

- 1-pound large strawberries

Directions:

1. Preheat the air fryer in Dehydrate mode at 110°F for 2 to 3 minutes. Use a mandolin slicer to thinly slice the strawberries. In batches, arrange a few of the strawberry pieces in a single layer on the cooking tray.
2. When the device is ready, move the cooking tray onto the top rack of the oven and close the oven
3. Set the timer to 7 minutes and press Start. Cook until the fruits are crispy.
4. Transfer the fruit chips to serving bowls when all set and make the remaining in the same manner. Delight in.

Nutrition:

- Calories: 36 kcal
- Fat: 0.34 g
- Carbs: 8.71 g
- Protein: 0.76 g

67. Chili Cheese Toasts

Basic Recipe

Preparation time: 5 minutes

Cooking Time: 10 minutes

Servings: 4

Ingredients:

- 1 teaspoon garlic powder
- 1 teaspoon red chili flakes
- 6 pieces sandwich bread
- 4 tablespoon butter
- 1 cup grated cheddar cheese
- 2 little fresh red chilies, deseeded and minced
- ½ teaspoon salt
- 1 tablespoon sliced fresh parsley

Directions:

1. Preheat the oven in Broil mode at 375°F for 2 to 3 minutes.
2. Spread the butter on one side of each bread piece and lay on a tidy, flat surface.
3. Divide the cheddar cheese on top and follow with the remaining ingredients. Lay 3 pieces of the bread on the cooking tray, slide the tray onto the middle rack of the oven and close the oven. Set the timer for 3 to 4 minutes and press Start. Cook till the cheese melts and is golden brown on top. Remove the first batch when ready and prepare the other three bread pieces. Slice them into triangle halves and serve immediately.

Nutrition:

- Calories: 105 kcal
- Fat: 11.53 g
- Carbs: 0.68 g
- Protein: 0.29 g

68. Cheese Sticks

Basic Recipe

Preparation time: 10 minutes

Cooking Time: 10 minutes

Servings: 6

Ingredients:

- 1 teaspoon garlic powder
- 1 teaspoon of Italian spices
- ¼ teaspoon rosemary, ground
- 2 eggs
- 1 cheese sticks
- ¼ cup parmesan cheese, grated
- ¼ cup whole-wheat flour

Directions:

1. Unwraps the cheese sticks. Keep aside. Beat the eggs into a bowl. Mix the cheese, flavorings, and flour in another bowl. Now roll the sticks in the egg and then into the batter. Coat well. Keep them in your air fryer basket. Cook for 7 minutes at 370°F. Serve hot.

Nutrition:

- Calories: 76 kcal
- Carbs: 5 g
- Fat: 4 g
- Protein: 5 g

69. Blended Veggie Chips

Basic Recipe

Preparation time: 20 minutes

Cooking Time: 10 minutes

Servings: 4

Ingredients:

- 1 big carrot
- 1 teaspoon salt
- 1 teaspoon Italian spices
- 1 zucchini
- 1 sweet potato peeled
- ½ teaspoon pepper
- 1 red beet, peeled
- A pinch cumin powder

Directions:

1. Preheat the air fryer in Dehydrate mode at 110°F for 2 to 3 minutes
2. Utilize a mandolin slicer to thinly slice all the vegetables and transfer them to a medium bowl. Season it with salt, Italian spices, and cumin powder. In batches, organize some of the veggies in a single layer on the cooking tray.
3. When the device is ready, move the cooking tray onto the top rack of the oven and close the oven, then set the timer to 7 or 9 minutes and press Start. Cook up until the veggies are crispy. Transfer the vegetables to serving bowls when all set and make them stay in the same manner. Delight in.

Nutrition:

- Calories: 84 kcal
- Fat: 0.15 g
- Carbs: 18.88 g
- Protein: 2.25 g

70. Sweet Apple and Pear Chips

Basic Recipe

Preparation time: 15 minutes

Cooking Time: 10 minutes

Servings: 4

Ingredients:

- 6 pears, peeled
- 6 Honey crisp apples

Directions:

1. Preheat the air fryer in Dehydrate mode at 110°F for 2 to 3 minutes. On the other hand, utilize a mandolin slicer to very finely slice the apples and pears. In batches, set up a few of the fruit slices in a single layer on the cooking tray.
2. When the device is ready, move the cooking tray onto the top rack of the oven and close the oven
3. Set the timer to 7 minutes and press Start. Cook till the fruits are crispy. Transfer the fruit chips to serving bowls when all set and make them stay in the same manner. Take pleasure in.

Nutrition:

- Calories: 142 kcal
- Fat: 0.46 g
- Carbs: 37.7 g
- Protein: 0.71 g

71. Cocoa Banana Chips

Basic Recipe

Preparation time: 5 minutes

Cooking Time: 7 minutes

Servings: 4

Ingredients:

- ¼ teaspoon cocoa powder
- 5 large firm bananas, peeled
- A cinnamon powder pinch

Directions:

1. Preheat the air fryer in Dehydrate mode at 110°F for 2 to 3 minutes. On the other hand, utilize a mandolin slicer to very finely slice the bananas and coat them well with cocoa powder and cinnamon powder. In batches, organize as many banana pieces as possible in a single layer on the cooking tray.
2. When the device is ready, slide the cooking tray onto the top rack of the oven and close the oven set the timer to 7 minutes, and press Start. Cook until the banana pieces are crispy. Transfer the chips to serving bowls when all set and make the remaining in the same manner. Take pleasure in.

Nutrition:

- Calories: 152 kcal
- Fat: 0.57 g
- Carbs: 38.89 g
- Protein: 1.87 g

72. Coriander Roasted Chickpeas

Basic Recipe

Preparation time: 10 minutes

Cooking Time: 45 minutes

Servings: 2

Ingredients:

- ¼ teaspoon garlic powder
- 1 (15 oz) can chickpeas, Dry-out pipes
- ¼ teaspoon ground coriander
- 1/8 teaspoon salt
- ¼ teaspoon chili pepper powder
- ¼ teaspoon curry powder
- ¼ teaspoon ground cumin
- ¼ teaspoon paprika
- Olive oil for spraying

Directions:

1. Preheat the oven in Air Fryer mode at 375°F for 2 to 3 minutes in a medium bowl, mix the chickpeas with all the spices until well-integrated, and pour into the rotisserie basket. Grease lightly with olive oil, shake the basket and close the seal. Fix the basket onto the lever in the oven and close the oven. Set the timer to 35 or 45 minutes, press Start, and cook up until the chickpeas are golden brown. After, open the oven, take out the basket utilizing the rotisserie lift and transfer the treat into serving bowls. Allow cooling and delight in.

Nutrition:

- Calories: 91 kcal
- Fat: 1.82 g
- Carbs: 14.87 g
- Protein: 4.61 g

Chapter 9 Appetizers

73. Egg Roll Wrapped with Cabbage and Prawns

Intermediate Recipe

Preparation time: 10 minutes

Cooking Time: 40 minutes

Servings: 4

Ingredients:

- 2 tablespoon vegetable oil
- 1-inch piece fresh ginger, grated
- 1 tablespoon minced garlic
- 1 carrot, cut into strips
- ¼ cup chicken broth
- 2 tablespoon reduced-sodium soy sauce
- 1 tablespoon sugar
- 1 cup shredded Napa cabbage
- 1 tablespoon sesame oil
- 8 cooked prawns, minced
- 1 egg
- 8 egg roll wrappers

Directions:

1. In a skillet over high heat, heat vegetable oil, and cook ginger and garlic for 40 seconds, until fragrant. Stir in carrot and cook for another 2 minutes. Pour in chicken broth, soy sauce, and sugar and bring to a boil.
2. Add cabbage and let simmer until softened, for 4 minutes. Remove the skillet from the heat and stir in sesame oil. Let cool for 15 minutes. Strain cabbage mixture, and fold in minced prawns. Whisk an egg in a small bowl. Fill each egg roll wrapper with prawn mixture, arranging the mixture just below the center of the wrapper.
3. Fold the bottom part over the filling and tuck under. Fold in both sides and tightly roll up. Use the whisked egg to seal the wrapper. Repeat until all egg rolls are ready. Place the rolls into a greased air fryer basket, spray them with oil and cook for 12 minutes at 370°F, turning once halfway through.

Nutrition:

- Calories: 215 kcal
- Fat: 7.9 g
- Carbs: 6.7 g
- Protein: 8 g

74. Sesame Garlic Chicken Wings

Intermediate Recipe

Preparation time: 10 minutes

Cooking Time: 40 minutes

Servings: 4

Ingredients:

- 1-pound chicken wings
- 1 cup soy sauce, divided
- ½ cup brown sugar
- ½ cup apple cider vinegar
- 2 tablespoons fresh ginger, minced
- 2 tablespoons fresh garlic, minced
- 1 teaspoon finely ground black pepper
- 2 tablespoon cornstarch
- 2 tablespoons cold water
- 1 teaspoon sesame seeds

Directions:

1. In a bowl, add chicken wings, and pour in half a cup soy sauce. Refrigerate for 20 minutes; Dry out and pat dry. Arrange the wings in the air fryer and cook for 30 minutes at 380°F, turning once halfway through. Make sure you check them towards the end to avoid overcooking.
2. In a skillet and over medium heat, stir sugar, half cup soy sauce, vinegar, ginger, garlic, and black pepper. Cook until sauce has reduced slightly, about 4 to 6 minutes
3. Dissolve 2 tablespoons of cornstarch in cold water in a bowl, and stir in the slurry into the sauce until it thickens; for 2 minutes, pour the sauce over wings and sprinkle with sesame seeds.

Nutrition:

- Calories: 413 kcal
- Fat: 8.3 g
- Carbs: 7 g
- Protein: 8.3 g

75. Savory Chicken Nuggets with Parmesan Cheese

Basic Recipe

Preparation time: 5 minutes

Cooking Time: 20 minutes

Servings: 4

Ingredients:

- 1 lb. chicken breast, boneless, skinless, cubed
- ½ teaspoon ground black pepper
- ¼ teaspoon kosher salt
- ¼ teaspoon seasoned salt
- 2 tablespoons olive oil
- 5 tablespoon plain breadcrumbs
- 2 tablespoon panko breadcrumbs
- 2 tablespoons grated Parmesan cheese

Directions:

1. Preheat the air fryer to 380°F and grease. Season the chicken with pepper, kosher salt, and seasoned salt; set aside. In a bowl, pour olive oil. In a separate bowl, add crumbs and Parmesan cheese.
2. Place the chicken pieces in the oil to coat, then dip into the breadcrumb mixture, and transfer to the air fryer. Work in batches if needed. Lightly spray chicken with cooking spray.
3. Cook the chicken for 10 minutes, flipping once halfway through. Cook until golden brown on the outside and no more pink on the inside.

Nutrition:

- Calories: 312 kcal
- Fat: 8.9 g
- Carbs: 7 g
- Protein: 10 g

76. Butternut Squash with Thyme

Basic Recipe

Preparation time: 5 minutes

Cooking Time: 20 minutes

Servings: 4

Ingredients:

- 2 cups peeled, butternut squash, cubed
- 1 tablespoon olive oil
- ¼ teaspoon salt
- ¼ teaspoon black pepper
- ¼ teaspoon dried thyme
- 1 tablespoon finely chopped fresh parsley

Directions:

1. In a bowl, add squash, oil, salt, pepper, and thyme, and toss until squash is well-coated.
2. Place squash in the air fryer and cook for 14 minutes at 360°F.
3. When ready, sprinkle with freshly chopped parsley and serve chilled.

Nutrition:

- Calories: 219 kcal
- Fat: 4.3 g
- Carbs: 9.4 g
- Protein: 7.8 g

77. Chicken Breasts in Golden Crumb

Basic Recipe

Preparation time: 10 minutes

Cooking Time: 25 minutes

Servings: 4

Ingredients:

- 1 ½ lb. chicken breasts, boneless, cut into strips
- 1 egg, lightly beaten
- 1 cup seasoned breadcrumbs
- Salt and black pepper to taste
- ½ teaspoon dried oregano

Directions:

1. Preheat the air fryer to 390°F. Season the chicken with oregano, salt, and black pepper. In a small bowl, whisk in some salt and pepper to the beaten egg. In a separate bowl, add the crumbs. Dip chicken tenders in the egg wash, then in the crumbs.
2. Roll the strips in the breadcrumbs and press firmly so the breadcrumbs stick well. Spray the chicken tenders with cooking spray and arrange them in the air fryer. Cook for 14 minutes, until no longer pink in the center and nice and crispy on the outside.

Nutrition:

- Calories: 223 kcal
- Fat: 3.2 g
- Carbs: 4.3 g
- Protein: 5 g

78. Yogurt Chicken Tacos

Basic Recipe

Preparation time: 5 minutes

Cooking Time: 20 minutes

Servings: 4

Ingredients:

- 1 cup cooked chicken, shredded
- 1 cup shredded mozzarella cheese
- ¼ cup salsa
- ¼ cup Greek yogurt
- Salt and ground black pepper
- 8 flour tortillas

Directions:

1. Mix chicken, cheese, salsa, and yogurt, and season with salt and pepper in a bowl. Spray one side of the tortilla with cooking spray. Lay 2 tablespoons of the chicken mixture at the center of the non-oiled side of each tortilla.
2. Roll tightly around the mixture. Arrange taquitos into your air fryer basket without overcrowding. Cook in batches if needed. Place the seam side down, or it will unravel during cooking crisps.
3. Cook it for 12 to 14 minutes, or until crispy, at 380°F.

Nutrition:

- Calories: 312 *kcal*
- Fat: 3 g
- Carbs: 6.5 g
- Protein: 6.2 g

79. Broccoli Salad with Goat Cheese

Basic Recipe

Preparation time: 10 minutes

Cooking Time: 10 minutes

Servings: 4

Ingredients:

- 2 ounces broccoli florets
- 3 onions
- 3 and 1/2 ounces of goat cheese
- 4 tomatoes, sliced
- 4 bell peppers
- Cooking spray
- Salt and pepper, to taste

Directions:

1. Use cooking spray to coat bell peppers, broccoli, and onions.
2. Preheat your air fry at 360°F in "AIR FRY" mode
3. Cook for 10 minutes.
4. Take a salad bowl and transfer the mixture into it.
5. Add goat cheese and tomatoes on top.
6. Then Season it with pepper and salt.
7. Serve and enjoy!

Nutrition:

- Calories: 380 kcal
- Fat: 15 g
- Carbs: 8 g
- Protein: 50 g

80. Juicy Fish Nuggets

Basic Recipe

Preparation time: 10 minutes

Cooking Time: 10 minutes

Servings: 4

Ingredients:

- 1-pound fresh cod
- 2 tablespoons olive oil
- 1/2 cup almond flour
- 2 large finely beaten eggs
- 1-2 cups almond meal
- Salt as needed

Directions:

1. Preheat your Air Fryer to 388°F in "AIR FRY" mode.
2. Take a food processor and add olive oil, almond meal, salt, and blend.
3. Take three bowls and add almond flour, almond meal, beaten eggs individually.
4. Take costs and cut them into slices of 1-inch thickness and 2-inch length.
5. Dredge slices into flour, eggs, and crumbs.
6. Transfer nuggets to the air fryer cooking basket and cook for 10 minutes until golden.
7. Serve and enjoy!

Nutrition:

- Calories: 200 kcal
- Fat: 14 g
- Carbs: 6 g
- Protein: 14 g

81. Vegetable Cutlets

Basic Recipe

Preparation time: 10 minutes

Cooking Time: 15 minutes

Servings: 6

Ingredients:

- 7 ounces potatoes
- 1/2 a carrot, grated
- 2 ounces capsicum, chopped
- 2 ounces cabbage, chopped
- Salt as needed
- Panko bread crumbs
- 1 teaspoon arrowroot mixed with water

Directions:

1. Take a pot of boiling water and add potatoes.
2. Once the potatoes are boiled, take them out and let them cool.
3. Peel the potatoes and mash them alongside cabbage capsicum, and season the mixture with salt.
4. Divide the mixture into 6 balls.
5. Flatten balls into cutlet shapes.
6. Coat each ball with arrowroot slurry and dredge them in breadcrumbs.
7. Preheat your Fryer to 356°F in "AIR FRY" mode.
8. Transfer balls to your Air Fryer cooking basket and cook for 8 minutes, give them a turn, and cook for 8 minutes more.
9. Serve and enjoy!

Nutrition:

- Calories: 240 kcal
- Fat: 4 g
- Carbs: 46 g
- Protein: 7 g

82. Cumin and Squash Chili

Basic Recipe

Preparation time: 10 minutes

Cooking Time: 16 minutes

Servings: 4

Ingredients:

- 1 medium butternut squash
- 2 teaspoons cumin seeds
- 1 large pinch of chili flakes
- 1 tablespoon olive oil
- and 1/2-ounces pine nuts
- 1 small bunch fresh coriander, chopped

Directions:

1. Take the squash and slice it. Remove seeds and cut them into smaller chunks
2. Take a bowl and add chunked squash, spice, and oil
3. Mix well
4. Preheat your Fryer to 360°F and add the squash to the cooking basket in "AIR FRY" mode
5. Roast for 20 minutes, making sure to shake the basket from time to time to avoid burning
6. Take a pan and place it over medium heat, add pine nuts to the pan, and dry toast for 2 minutes
7. Sprinkle nuts on top of the squash and serve
8. Enjoy!

Nutrition:

- Calories: 400 kcal
- Fat: 15 g
- Carbs: 50 g
- Protein: 16 g

83. Banana Fritters

Basic Recipe

Preparation time: 10 minutes

Cooking Time: 16 minutes

Servings: 6

Ingredients:

- 1 medium butternut squash
- 2 teaspoons cumin seeds
- 1 large pinch of chili flakes
- 1 tablespoon olive oil
- and 1/2-ounces pine nuts
- 1 small bunch of fresh coriander, chopped

Directions:

1. Preheat your Air Fryer to 340°F in "AIR FRY" mode.
2. Take a bowl and add salt, sesame seeds, water, and mix them well until a nice batter forms.
3. Coat the bananas with the flour mixture and transfer them to the fryer basket.
4. Cook for 8 minutes.
5. Enjoy!

84. Onion Pakora

Basic Recipe

Preparation time: 10 minutes

Cooking Time: 10 minutes

Servings: 4

Ingredients:

- 1 cup Gram Flour
- 1/4 cup almond flour
- 2 teaspoons olive oil
- 4 whole onions
- 2 green chili
- 1 tablespoon coriander
- 1/4 teaspoon carom
- 1/8 teaspoon chili powder
- Salt as needed

Directions:

1. Slice your onion into individual slices.
2. Chop the green chilies.
3. Cut up the coriander into equal-sized portions.
4. Take a bowl and add carom, turmeric powder, salt, and chili powder.
5. Add onion, chilies, and coriander.
6. Mix well.
7. Add water and keep mixing until you have a dough-like consistency.
8. Mix the dough and form balls.
9. Preheat your Fryer to 392°F in "AIR FRY" mode.
10. Cook for 8 minutes.
11. Make sure to keep checking after every 6 minutes to ensure that they are not burnt.

Nutrition:

- Calories: 280 kcal
- Fat: 20 g
- Carbs: 28 g
- Protein: 8 g

85. Lemon Green Beans

Basic Recipe

Preparation time: 10 minutes

Cooking Time: 12-15 minutes

Servings: 4

Ingredients:

- 1-pound green beans washed and de-stemmed
- 1 lemon
- Pinch salt
- 1/4 teaspoon oil

Directions:

1. Add beans to your Air Fryer cooking basket.
2. Squeeze a few drops of lemon.
3. Season it with salt and pepper.
4. Drizzle with olive oil on top.
5. Cook for 10-12 minutes at 400°F in "AIR FRY" mode.
6. Once done, serve and enjoy!

Nutrition:

- Calories: 90 kcal
- Fat: 5 g
- Carbs: 9 g
- Protein: 2 g

86. Coconut Muffins

Basic Recipe

Preparation time: 5 minutes

Cooking Time: 25 minutes

Servings: 5

Ingredients:

- ½ cup coconut flour
- 2 tablespoons cocoa powder
- 3 tablespoons Erythritol
- 1 teaspoon baking powder
- 2 tablespoons coconut oil
- 2 eggs, beaten
- ½ cup coconut shred

Nutrition:

- Calories: 206 kcal
- Fat: 16.7 g
- Fiber: 7.1 g
- Carbs: 13 g
- Protein: 4.2 g

87. Coffee Muffins

Basic Recipe

Preparation time: 10 minutes

Cooking Time: 11 minutes

Servings: 6

- 1 teaspoon vanilla extract
- 1 teaspoon instant coffee
- 1 teaspoon baking powder
- 1 egg, beaten
- ¼ cup Erythritol

Ingredients:

- 1 cup coconut flour

Directions:

1. Mix coconut flour with coconut oil, vanilla extract, instant coffee, baking powder, egg, and Erythritol.
2. Put the mixture in the muffin molds and cook in the air fryer at 375°F for 11 minutes.

Nutrition:

- Calories: 172 kcal
- Fat: 11.8 g
- Fiber: 8 g
- Carbs: 13.9 g
- Protein: 3.6 g

88. Almond Cookies

Basic Recipe

Preparation time: 5 minutes

Cooking Time: 15 minutes

Servings: 8

Ingredients:

- ½ teaspoon baking powder
- 5 tablespoons coconut oil, softened
- 1 cup almond flour
- 2 oz almonds, grinded
- 2 tablespoons Erythritol
- ½ teaspoon vanilla extract

Directions:

1. Mix almond flour with almonds, Erythritol, baking powder, coconut oil, and vanilla extract. Knead the dough.
2. Make the small cookies and place them in the air fryer basket.
3. Cook the cookies at 350°F for 15 minutes.

Nutrition:

- Calories: 199 kcal
- Fat: 18.7 g
- Fiber 2.4 g
- Carbs: 4.7 g
- Protein: 4.5 g

89. Thumbprint Cookies

Basic Recipe

Preparation time: 15 minutes

Cooking Time: 9 minutes

Servings: 6

Ingredients:

- 2 teaspoons coconut oil, softened
- 1 tablespoon Erythritol
- 1 egg, beaten
- ½ cup coconut flour
- 1 oz almonds, chopped

Directions:

1. Mix all ingredients in the mixing bowl. Knead the dough.
2. Then make cookies from the dough and put them in the air fryer basket.
3. Cook the cookies at 365°F for 9 minutes.

Nutrition:

- Calories: 91 kcal
- Fat: 5.6 g
- Fiber: 4.6 g
- Carbs: 10.2 g
- Protein: 3.3 g

90. Pecan Bars

Basic Recipe

Preparation time: 5 minutes

Cooking Time: 40 minutes

Servings: 12

Ingredients:

- 2 cups coconut flour
- 5 tablespoons Erythritol
- 4 tablespoons coconut oil, softened
- ½ cup heavy cream
- 1 egg, beaten
- 4 pecans, chopped

Directions:

1. Mix coconut flour, Erythritol, coconut oil, heavy cream, and egg.
2. Pour the batter into the air fryer basket and flatten well.
3. Top the mixture with pecans and cook the meal at 350°F for 40 minutes.
4. Cut the cooked meal into the bars.

Nutrition:

- Calories: 174 kcal
- Fat: 12.1 g
- Fiber: 8.5 g
- Carbs: 14.2 g
- Protein: 3.7 g

91. Brown Muffins

Basic Recipe

Preparation time: 15 minutes

Cooking Time: 10 minutes

Servings: 2

Ingredients:

- 1 egg, beaten
- 1 tablespoon coconut oil, softened
- 2 tablespoons almond flour
- 1 tablespoon cocoa powder
- 1 tablespoon Erythritol
- 1 teaspoon ground cinnamon

Directions:

1. Mix egg with coconut oil, almond flour, cocoa powder, Erythritol, and ground cinnamon.
2. Pour the muffin batter into the muffin molds.
3. Bake the muffins at 375°F for 10 minutes.

Nutrition:

- Calories: 141 kcal
- Fat: 12.7 g
- Fiber: 2.2 g
- Carbs: 4.1 g
- Protein: 4.8 g

92. Lime Bars

Basic Recipe

Preparation time: 10 minutes

Cooking Time: 35 minutes

Servings: 10

Ingredients:

- 3 tablespoons coconut oil, melted
- 3 tablespoons Splenda
- 1 ½ cup coconut flour
- 3 eggs, beaten
- 1 teaspoon lime zest, grated
- 3 tablespoons lime juice

Directions:

1. Cover the air fryer basket bottom with baking paper.
2. Then in the mixing bowl, mix Splenda with coconut flour, eggs, lime zest, and lime juice.
3. Pour the mixture into the air fryer basket and flatten gently.
4. Cook the meal at 350°F for 35 minutes.
5. Then cool the cooked meal a little and cut it into bars.

Nutrition:

- Calories: 144 kcal
- Fat: 7.2 g
- Fiber: 7.2 g
- Carbs: 15.7 g
- Protein: 4.1 g

93. Tender Macadamia Bars

Basic Recipe

Preparation time: 15 minutes

Cooking Time: 30 minutes

Servings: 10

Ingredients:

- 3 tablespoons butter, softened
- 1 teaspoon baking powder
- 1 teaspoon apple cider vinegar
- 1 cup coconut flour
- 3 tablespoons swerve
- 1 teaspoon vanilla extract
- 2 eggs, beaten
- 2 oz macadamia nuts, chopped
- Cooking spray

Directions:

1. Spray the air fryer basket with cooking spray.
2. Then mix all remaining ingredients in the mixing bowl and stir until you get a homogenous mixture.
3. Pour the mixture into the air fryer basket and cook at 345°F for 30 minutes.
4. When the mixture is cooked, cut it into bars and transfer it to the serving plates.

Nutrition:

- Calories: 158 kcal
- Fat: 10.4 g
- Fiber: 7.7 g
- Carbs: 13.1 g
- Protein: 4 g

94. Vanilla Pie

Basic Recipe

Preparation time: 10 minutes

Cooking Time: 40 minutes

Servings: 8

Ingredients:

- ½ cup coconut cream
- 3 eggs, beaten
- 1 tablespoon vanilla extract
- 1 teaspoon baking powder
- 3 tablespoons swerve
- 1 cup coconut flour
- 1 tablespoon coconut oil, melted

Directions:

1. Mix coconut cream with eggs, vanilla extract, baking powder, swerve, coconut flour, and coconut oil.
2. Then transfer the mixture to the air fryer basket and flatten it gently.
3. Cook the pie at 355°F for 40 minutes.

Nutrition:

- Calories: 139 kcal
- Fat: 8.9 g
- Fiber: 5.3 g
- Carbs: 9.5 g
- Protein: 4.4 g

95. Soft Turmeric Cookies

Basic Recipe

Preparation time: 10 minutes

Cooking Time: 20 minutes

Servings: 12

Ingredients:

- 2 eggs, beaten
- 1 tablespoon coconut cream
- 3 tablespoons coconut oil, melted
- 2 teaspoons ground turmeric
- 1 teaspoon vanilla extract
- 2.5 cup coconut flour
- 2 tablespoons Erythritol

Directions:

1. Mix all ingredients in the mixing bowl.
2. Knead the dough and make the cookies using the cutter.
3. Put the cookies in the air fryer basket and cook at 350°F for 20 minutes.

Nutrition:

- Calories: 147 kcal
- Fat: 17 g
- Fiber: 10.1 g
- Carbs: 17.6 g

96. Vanilla Scones

Basic Recipe

Preparation time: 20 minutes

Cooking Time: 10 minutes

Servings: 6

Ingredients:

- ¼ cup heavy cream
- 1 teaspoon vanilla extract
- 1 tablespoon Erythritol

- Cooking spray

- 4 oz coconut flour
- ½ teaspoon baking powder
- 1 teaspoon apple cider vinegar
- 2 teaspoons mascarpone

Directions:

1. In the mixing bowl, mix coconut flour with baking powder, apple cider vinegar, mascarpone, heavy cream, vanilla extract, and Erythritol.
2. Knead the dough and cut it into scones.
3. Then put them in the air fryer basket and sprinkle with cooking spray.
4. Cook the vanilla scones at 365°F for 10 minutes.

Nutrition:

- Calories: 104 kcal
- Fat: 4.1 g
- Fiber: 8.1 g
- Carbs: 14 g
- Protein: 3 g

97. Mint Pie

Basic Recipe

Preparation time: 15 minutes

Cooking Time: 25 minutes

Servings: 2

Ingredients:

- 1 tablespoon instant coffee
- 2 tablespoons almond butter, softened
- 2 tablespoons Erythritol
- 1 teaspoon dried mint
- 3 eggs, beaten
- 1 teaspoon spearmint, dried
- 4 teaspoons coconut flour
- Cooking spray

Directions:

1. Spray the air fryer basket with cooking spray.
2. Then mix all ingredients in the mixer bowl.
3. When you get a smooth mixture, transfer it to the air fryer basket. Flatten it gently.
4. Cook the pie at 365°F for 25 minutes.

Nutrition:

- Calories: 313 kcal
- Fat: 19.6 g
- Fiber: 11.7 g
- Carbs: 19.6 g
- Protein: 15.7 g

98. Saffron Cookies

Basic Recipe

Preparation time: 10 minutes

Cooking Time: 15 minutes

Servings: 12

- 1 egg, beaten
- 2 teaspoons saffron
- 1 teaspoon vanilla extract

Ingredients:

- 2 cups coconut flour
- ½ cup Erythritol
- ¼ cup coconut, melted

Directions:

1. Mix all ingredients in the bowl and knead the dough.
2. Make the cookies and put them in the air fryer basket in one layer.
3. Cook the cookies at 355°F for 15 minutes.

Nutrition:

- Calories: 106 kcal
- Fat: 4.3 g
- Fiber: 8.2 g
- Carbs: 12.4 g
- Protein: 4.5 g

99. Keto Balls

Intermediate Recipe

Preparation time: 15 minutes

Cooking Time: 4 minutes

Servings: 10

Ingredients:

- 2 eggs, beaten
- 1 teaspoon coconut oil, melted
- 9 oz coconut flour
- 5 oz provolone cheese, shredded
- 2 tablespoons Erythritol
- 1 teaspoon baking powder
- ¼ teaspoon ground coriander
- Cooking spray

Directions:

1. Mix eggs with coconut oil, coconut flour, Provolone cheese, Erythritol, baking powder, and ground cinnamon.
2. Make the balls and put them in the air fryer basket.
3. Sprinkle the balls with cooking spray and cook at 400°F for 4 minutes.

Nutrition:

- Calories: 176 kcal
- Fat: 7.8 g
- Fiber: 10.9 g
- Carbs: 18.9 g
- Protein: 8.4 g

100. Sage Muffins

Intermediate Recipe

Preparation time: 10 minutes

Cooking Time: 20 minutes

Servings: 8

Ingredients:

- 3 tablespoons coconut oil, softened
- 1 egg, beaten
- ½ cup Erythritol
- ¼ cup almond flour
-
- 1 teaspoon dried sage
- 3 tablespoons mascarpone
- ½ teaspoon baking soda
- Cooking spray

Directions:

1. Spray the muffin molds with cooking spray.
2. Then mix all ingredients in the mixing bowl and stir until smooth.
3. Pour the mixture into the muffin molds and transfer it to the air fryer.
4. Cook the muffins at 350°F for 20 minutes.

Nutrition:

- Calories: 85 kcal
- Fat: 8.3 g
- Fiber: 0.4 g
- Carbs: 0.9 g
- Protein: 1.4 g

Conclusion

A quick and easy way to cook crispy and delicious food without a lot of the hassle that comes with deep frying, air fryers use dry oil or hot air to circulate around the food in a small, enclosed space like how it would be cooked traditionally at home.

The Air Fryer is a fantastic gadget that is simple to use and can provide the ultimate home cooking experience. As a result of this, every time you use this device, you'll be able to eat healthy and delicious cuisine.

These days, health is one of the most popular cooking tactics, and air fryers have become one of the most useful kitchen appliances.

You must have an air fryer and this wonderful air fryer cookbook!

I hope you find this one-of-a-kind cookbook useful in your quest to become a better version of yourself! There are various ways to improve your physical life, which spills over into other areas as well.

Its high-efficiency heating technique can provide golden, crispy meals that may be made at home. Users can now choose from 11 innovative programs depending on their culinary needs.

You have more options for preparing your food in a free and enjoyable manner, with less oil, natural and crispy fats on the exterior, and juices on the inside. Remember that if you know how to cook, the steps for preparing dishes may differ. You will find the best tastes for your recipes if the proportions of the components provided are obeyed, and your adventure into using an air fryer will substantially reduce unhealthy, fried foods.

You'll find a new flavor with the air fryer, but it'll be very close to what you're used to. The amount of Fat: in your dish is the only substantial difference the air fryer creates. Invest in an air fryer and devote time to becoming a better version of yourself in order to extend your life.

If you enjoy cooking and are a foodie, this is the finest tool for you to purchase. It allows you to change the temperature and settings as needed. With its excellent performance, it produces outstanding results.

If you want to be in shape, you'll have to give up fast food and junk food because that's no way to feed the one body you'll ever have. I hope the chapters you've just finished will assist you in achieving your objectives, whatever they may be.

The next step is to put what you've learned into practice in your daily life! Choose a few dishes that appeal to you and make it a goal to cook and enjoy them as a first step toward a healthier lifestyle.

You'll soon be creating the most effective dishes ever, and your home poached meals will impress everyone around you!

Just put your faith in us! Start your new change of state adventure with your hands-on associate.

A

B

C

O

E

F

G

H

J

K

L

N

P

R

S

T

V

Y

Z

Printed in Great Britain
by Amazon

25821033R00053